PRO-EARTH

FRIENDSHIP PRESS • NEW YORK

Unless otherwise stated, all Bible quotations used in this book are from the Revised Standard Version, copyright 1946 and 1952 by the Division of Christian Education of the National Council of the Churches of Christ in the United States of America. Such quotations have in certain instances been edited for inclusive language concerns according to that organization's guidelines.

ISBN 0-377-00154-6

Editorial offices: 475 Riverside Drive, Room 772, New York NY 10115
Distribution offices: P.O. Box 37844, Cincinnati, OH 45237
Copyright © 1985 Friendship Press, Inc.
Printed in the United States of America

CONTENTS

CARING FOR GOD'S EARTH

"THE LAND IS SACRED TO US"
Chief Seattle's Lament 3

LOVING CREATION
By Douglas John Hall 5

WATER

WATER—THE MOST ESSENTIAL RESOURCE
By Richard J. Barnet 9

"WHEN THE WELL'S DRY..."
Water News from Around the World ... 15

LAND

LAND, PEOPLE, CHANGE
By B. David Williams 21

THIS LAND IS HOME TO US
By David Liden 22

WHERE HAVE ALL THE BLACK FARMERS GONE?
By Joseph F. Brooks 26

DOMINATING THE LAND
Land News from Around the World ... 28

CULTIVATING THE EARTH

A LETTER TO THE CHURCHES
By David L. Ostendorf 33

FARMING, BENSON-STYLE
By Bob Shoemake 38

PESTICIDES—A GLOBAL AFFAIR 40
Tasty But Toxic 40
Pesticides and the Third World
By David Weir 42
A Non-chemical Alternative
By Linda Siskind 44

THE LAND MOURNS

CREATION SUFFERS
The Plague of Acid Rain 47

POISONS IN THE EARTH
By Deborah A. Sheiman 53

Is There a Dump in Your Backyard? .. 56

THE SEARCH FOR A NEW BOWL AND SALT
By James N. Brewster 58

How Churches Responded to Love Canal 60

AFTER THE URANIUM SPILL
By Barbara H. Chase 61

Churches' Response to Non-natural Disasters 63

How to Make Hard Decisions about Energy 64

A VISION OF LIFE IN ALL ITS FULLNESS

THE SEARCH FOR A NEW HUMILITY
By William E. Gibson 66

LAND AND MILITARIZATION 71

MARSHALL ISLANDS MON AMOUR
By Darlene Keju-Johnson 72

The Heritage of Atomic Tests 74

CHANGING OUR LIFESTYLES
By Earl Arnold 75

STEWARDSHIP AND ECONOMICS
By William E. Gibson 77

"GOD'S VOICE IS THE VOICE OF ALL NATURE"
By Cecil Corbett 80

LEADERS' GUIDES

"CARING FOR GOD'S EARTH"—A GUIDE FOR LEADERS
By Carolyn Hardin Engelhardt 83

YOUTH LEADER'S GUIDE
By Fred Coulter 92

RESOURCES 97

PREFACE

This is a book about the earth. It's about people who from the beginning of human history have revered the earth and sung its praises, sowed and harvested it and tapped its power. The book is also about those who have parcelled out the earth, sapped its resources, upset its balance and detached themselves from its mysteries. And the book is about God, who made the earth for everyone, who continues to stir human beings to justice and compassion.

The readings in PRO-EARTH are drawn from newspaper articles and church publications, environmental journals and personal reflections. They focus on two crucial questions: Who should have access to the land and its resources? How can we take care of the earth so that its ability to sustain life is not irreparably damaged?

The issues raised are timely and immediate. Hardly a day went by during the editing of the book that a news story did not call attention to water shortages in the Western states, to the rapid increase in soil erosion, to the economic crisis faced by Midwestern farmers or to new findings about acid rain in Canada. Years of famine in Africa began to make headlines. The implications of manufacturing hazardous substances in developing countries dominated the news for weeks after the tragedy in Bhopal.

Signs of hope emerged as well. Across the world, people were admitting that technological "progress" might have limits after all. There were reports of neighbors getting together to stop proposed toxic waste dumps in their communities; of Pacific islanders resisting the use of their homes as testing sites for nuclear weapons; of subsistence farmers in developing countries supporting their families with small amounts of land and equipment; of churches educating congregations about the politics of clean air. North Americans continued to look hard at their own patterns of consumption, increasingly aware that their own comfortable lifestyles are supported by international systems that may be endangering the earth and supporting the oppression of many of its peoples.

The book does not claim to cover every contemporary environmental concern. What it does offer is a starting-point for understanding the biblical vision of humanity in relation to God's earth—and how current environmental situations connect with this vision. Many of the biblical references are striking in their immediacy. On the use of land, for instance. Benton Rhoades, director of Agricultural Missions for the National Council of Churches of Christ in the U.S.A., refers to Leviticus 26:3 when he writes that "landlessness and land abuse are aberations from life as it is meant to be. . .the epitome of broken relationships." A good point to consider when questioning why so many Appalachians have lost control of their land or why toxic wastes continue to be buried in the earth without adequate safety precautions. Or consider the gross imbalance between the ability of the rich and the poor to benefit from Creation's gifts; the ancient words of Amos and Hosea speak directly to our 20th century denial of God's trust.

PRO-EARTH. As the title implies, we have a choice. We can be for the earth or indifferent to it. To be *for* the earth, however, requires more than respect for the Bible's teachings. It requires new "eyes to see" what stewardship demands of us now. It means being conversant with the facts in local and global environmental situations and carefully considering options for action. It means following and influencing whatever political legislation will affect the future of the earth. It means being aware of, and supporting, grassroots efforts to intervene in patterns of consumption and disposal that lead to the abuse of the earth. It requires nothing less than a "renewing" of our minds. (Romans 12:2)

It is no accident that PRO-EARTH begins and ends with the words of Native people, whose experience of the earth could only lead them to walk gently upon it and to share its gifts. As North Americans we must see this as part of our heritage, for the earth that sustains us today depends on us for its very survival. The good relationship *can* be restored; that is the faith in which this book has been compiled.

—Nadine Hundertmark
Editor

CARING FOR GOD'S EARTH

And God saw everything that was made, and behold, it was very good.

"THE LAND IS SACRED TO US"
Chief Seattle's Lament – 1854

The Great Chief in Washington sends word that he wishes to buy our land. The Great Chief also sends us words of friendship and goodwill. This is kind of him, since we know he has little need for our friendship in return. But we will consider your offer. For we know that if we do not sell, the white man may come with guns and take our land.

How can you buy or sell the sky, the warmth of the land? The idea is strange to us.

If we do not own the freshness of the air and the sparkle of the water, how can you buy them?

Every part of this earth is sacred to my people. Every shining pine needle, every sandy shore, every mist in the dark woods, every clearing, and humming insect is holy in the memory and experience of my people. The sap which courses through the trees carries the memories of the red man.

The white man's dead forget the country of their birth when they go to walk among the stars. Our dead never forget this beautiful earth, for it is the mother of the red man. We are part of the earth and it is part of us. The perfumed flowers are our sisters; the deer, the horse, the great eagle, these are our brothers. The rocky crests, the juices in the meadows, the body heat of the pony, and man — all belong to the same family.

So, when the Great Chief in Washington sends word that he wishes to buy our land, he asks much of us. The Great Chief sends word he will reserve us a place so that we can live comfortably to ourselves. He will be our father and we will be his children. So we will consider your offer to buy our land. But it will not be easy. For this land is sacred to us.

The red man has always retreated before the advancing white man, as the mist of the mountain runs before the morning sun. But the ashes of our fathers are sacred. Their graves are holy ground, and so these hills, these trees, this portion of the earth is consecrated to us. We know that the white man does not understand our ways. One portion of land is the same to him as the next, for he is a stranger who comes in the night and takes from the land whatever he needs. The earth is not his brother, but his enemy, and when he has conquered it, he moves on. He leaves his fathers' graves behind, and he does not care. He kidnaps the earth from his children. He does not care. His fathers' graves and his children's birthright are forgotten. He treats his mother, the earth, and his brother, the sky, as things to be bought, plundered, sold like sheep or bright beads. His appetite will devour the earth and leave behind only a desert.

I do not know. Our ways are different from your ways. The sight of your cities pains the eyes of the red man. But perhaps it is because the red man is a savage and does not understand.

There is no quiet place in the white man's cities. No place to hear the unfurling of leaves in spring or the rustle of insect's wings. But perhaps it is because I am a savage and do not understand. The clatter only seems to insult the ears. And what is there to life if a man cannot hear the lonely cry of the whippoorwill or the arguments of the frogs around a pond at night? I am a red man and do not understand. The Indian prefers the soft sound of the wind darting over the face of a pond and the smell of the wind itself, cleansed by a midday rain or scented with the pinon pine.

The air is precious to the red man, for all things share the same breath — the beast, the tree, the man, they all share the same breath. The white man does not seem to notice the air he breaths. Like a man dying for many days, he is numb to the stench. But if we sell you our land, you must remember that the air is precious to us, that the air shares its spirit with all the life it supports. The wind that gave our grandfather his first breath also receives his last sigh. And the wind must also give our children the spirit of life. And if we sell you our land, you must keep it apart and sacred, as a place where even the white man can go to taste the wind that is sweetened by the meadow's flowers.

So we will consider your offer to buy our land. If we decide to accept, I will make one condition: The white man must treat the beasts of this land as his brothers.

I am a savage and I do not understand any other way. I have seen a thousand rotting buffalos on the prairie, left by the white man who shot them from a passing

---

Chief Sealth of the Duwamish League, known to us as Chief Seattle, delivered this speech in 1854—one year before a great treaty-making council was held between fourteen Indian tribes and the U.S. Government. The government proposed that reservations be established, and although several tribes opposed this, treaties were signed: each of the fourteen tribes was to select its favorite home valley as its reservation. Three months later, war broke out. The conflict lasted three years and broke Indian strength in the Northwest. Ironically, Sealth was a strong American ally throughout. Little else is known of his life.

train. I am a savage and I do not understand how the smoking iron horse can be more important than the buffalo that we kill only to stay alive.

What is man without the beasts? If all the beasts were gone, men would die from a great loneliness of spirit. For whatever happens to the beasts, soon happens to man. All things are connected.

So we will consider your offer to buy our land. If we agree, it will be to secure the reservation you have promised. There, perhaps, we may live out our brief days as we wish. When the last red man has vanished from this earth, and his memory is only the shadow of a cloud moving across the prairie, these shores and forests will still hold the spirits of my people. For they love this earth as the newborn loves its mother's heartbeat. So if we sell you our land, love it as we've loved it. Care for it as we've cared for it. Hold in your mind the memory of the land as it is when you take it. And with all your strength, with all your mind, with all your heart, preserve it for your children, and love it...as God loves us all.

One thing we know, Our God is the same God. This earth is precious to Him. Even the white man cannot be exempt from the common destiny. We may be brothers after all. We shall see.

This we know: The earth does not belong to man; man belongs to the earth. This we know: All things are connected like the blood which unites one family. All things are connected.

Whatever befalls the earth befalls the sons of the earth. Man did not weave the web of life; he is merely a strand in it. Whatever he does to the web, he does to himself.

But we will consider your offer to go to the reservation you have for my people. We will live apart, and in peace. It matters little where we spend the rest of our days. Our children have seen their fathers humbled in defeat. Our warriors have felt shame, and after defeat they turn their days in idleness and contaminate their bodies with sweet foods and strong drink. It matters little where we pass the rest of our days. Tribes are made of men, nothing more. Men come and go like waves of the sea.

Even the white man, whose God walks and talks with him as friend to friend, cannot be exempt from the common destiny. We may be brothers after all; we shall see. One thing we know, which the white man may one day discover — our God is the same God. You may think now that you own Him as you wish to own our land; but you cannot. He is the God of man, and His compassion is equal for the red man and the white. This earth is precious to Him, and to harm the earth is to heap contempt on its Creator. The whites too shall pass; perhaps sooner than all other tribes. Continue to contaminate your bed, and you will one night suffocate in your own waste.

But in your perishing you will shine brightly, fired by the strength of the God who brought you to this land and for some special purpose gave you dominion over this land and over the red man. Your destiny is a mystery to us, for we do not understand when the buffalo are all slaughtered, the wild horses are tamed, the secret corners of the forest heavy with the scent of many men, and the view of the ripe hills blotted by talking wires. Where is the thicket? Gone. Where is the eagle? Gone. And what is it to say goodbye to the swift pony and the hunt? The end of living and the beginning of survival.

LOVING CREATION

God made us stewards of Creation, not dominators.
But Christian tradition has not always made this relationship clear.

by Douglas John Hall

"Nature is the enemy! She must be brought to her knees!" Such were the triumphant words of the narrator of an unforgettable documentary film I saw some decades ago. The screen showed us a vast upheaval, an explosion caused (one supposes) by tons of dynamite: rocks and trees and water and, in all likelihood, thousands of little animals went rushing pell-mell heavenwards. And when the dust settled, there were the earth-movers and the heavy machinery ready to turn the wilderness of the North into one of the great hydroelectric projects of our continent. This undertaking, the actual need and worth of which has been seriously challenged by scientists, economists and politicians, is a monument to the technocratic mentality.

But what was so vexing to me as I watched the film was that the same script that identified nature as "the enemy" was studded with quotations from the Bible. What are we to make of this? Is biblical faith guilty of aiding the industrial oppression of the natural world with its too-lofty estimation of the human species and its frank denigration of the animal and vegetable kingdoms? How are we to reconcile the apparent contradictions of a religion that clearly makes God's "good" creation the object of God's love...and then seems to give to greedy humans all the justification they need for turning the beautiful place God made into a pigsty?

In my response to this question I shall consider three possible ways of thinking about the relationship between humanity and nature: humanity *above* nature, humanity *in* nature, and humanity *with* nature.

HUMANITY *ABOVE* NATURE

This perspective places *Homo sapiens* on a very high rung of the ladder of being and insists that "nature" is simply there for us to use. At the outset of the Modern period, Western philosophy was crammed full of this

---

Douglas John Hall is Professor of Christian Theology at McGill University in Montreal. He is the author of Christian Mission: The Stewardship of Life in the Kingdom of Death *(Friendship Press, 1985) and numerous other books. This article is adapted from a paper titled, "Stewardship as Key to a Theology of Nature."*

sentiment. As the English philosopher Thomas Hobbes wrote, overcoming the Medieval tendency to regard nature cautiously, as a realm of immense mystery: "She is no mystery, for she worketh by motion and geometry...(and we) can chart these motions."

This has been the dominant attitude from the beginning of the Modern era into our own time. And we, today, are part of a society that has been built upon this premise. The idea that humanity is nature's "lord and possessor," capable of making over what God rather thoughtlessly put together in the first place, is an almost exact description of the North American attitude towards the natural universe. It is our very birthright.

But is this attitude really a by-product of the Judao-Christian tradition? I don't think so. There are many elements of the biblical tradition that go against the grain of such a manipulative approach to nature. For example, the Bible associates such manipulation *not* with the will of God, but rather with human disobedience. When human beings sin, nature suffers, as the following passage from Isaiah 24 reveals:

> The earth mourns and withers,
>   the world languishes and withers;
>   the heavens languish together with the
>   earth.
> The earth lies polluted
>   under its inhabitants;
> For they have transgressed the laws,
>   violated the statutes,
>   broken the everlasting covenant.

The real roots of the "humanity above nature" complex, I believe, are not in Christianity *per se*, but in the mixture of post-Medieval Christianity and Renaissance humanism that appeared on the European scene about the time Columbus took it upon himself to master the Atlantic Ocean.

Still, one must ask: Why did Christians then and now permit Christianity to be used in this way? Why have Christians continued to pronounce "Christian truth" with so little regard for the manner in which it was being heard and used? For example, the concept that humans are created "in the image of God" has readily supported the idea of "humanity above nature." Had Christian theologians been more atuned to the biblical text from which this concept comes, they might have learned that the "image of God" does not refer to a quality we possess at all. It does not make us so much better than the other creatures. Instead, it refers to the relationship in which we stand *vis à vis* our Creator. This is a relationship that makes us responsible for and representative of the others. Stewards of them, let us say. But more on that later.

HUMANITY *IN* NATURE
That is, think of human beings as one of the myriad creatures, nothing more, one species among the others, as mortal, as dependent, having no more to offer and no more right to life than anything else. This conception is also a Modern one, but we also discover hints of it in Scripture, when the character and destiny of the human creature is compared to that of all the others:

> All flesh is grass,
>   and all its beauty is like the flower
>   of the field.
> The grass withers, the flower fades,
>   when the breath of the Lord blows upon it;
> surely the people is grass.
>
> (Isaiah 40)

Yet in the Bible, humanity is hardly ever just "grass." There is a mystery about this human creature, a mystery of mind, of spirit. "Humanity *in* nature" is a reaction against the spirit of the Enlightenment and the industrialization that flowed out of it. The Romantics were rebelling on the side of the "heart" on the side of nature. From Rousseau onwards, they fought against the modern world's rationalistic reduction of humanity. For they saw, quite rightly, that this supposed elevation of the human species above nature was at the same time a denigration of the species, turning humanity into nothing but brain.

They did not err in their judgement. The technocrats are providing us with foolproof methods for dispensing with all the unpredictable, messy elements of human life. "Science is power" has come to mean power over the human species, too!

But sometimes the pendulum of history swings too far. Extremes beget extremes. And we find ourselves caught between one absurd reduction and another. So it is now possible to hear even Christians speaking as if the only way of saving the planet were for the human species to plan itself out of existence. . . to become as "natural" as the dinosaurs! Now, there is no doubt that the human species has created more trouble in the world than any other creature. But is the healing of creation to be achieved though the extinction of this troublesome creature? Not as I read the story of our redemption!

HUMANITY *WITH* NATURE
This is, without doubt, the vision that flows through our Judao-Christian tradition. Humanity *with* nature. Not above it. Not merely in it. But with it. "With" contains both the idea of sameness and the idea of difference. To put it more succinctly, "with" is the preposition that belongs to the language of love. Love means, "I am *with* you and you are *with* me in a special sense. We evoke each other's potential for being.''Our being as human beings is a being *with*. And the distortion of sin is precisely our alienation from all that we are created to be *with*. Sin is being alone; being against.

But Christian theology has rarely explored the meaning of these fundamental assumptions when it has considered our relationship to the non-human world. This is what must now be explored.

According to the biblical witness, we *are* different. Different does not mean superior. It means that we are more complex, more versatile, and certainly more vulnerable than the other parts of God's creation. But why? Not so that we can lord it over them! Rather, so that we can exercise our unique *responsibility towards* them—our unique *answerability for* them. We are to "have dominion."

But what does that mean? Who, biblically-speaking, is our model of "dominion"? Is it Caesar? Pharoah? No, it is the one whom we call "Lord"—Jesus the Christ. . ."and him crucified." His dominion, far from being a trampling over everybody and everything, seems to have involved his being trampled upon.

So yes, we are different from the beasts of the field and the birds of the air. Let us not be romantic and imagine that we can just melt into nature. We have a reflective side that the other creatures do not have. It is harder for us to die than it is for them. We have always to choose or to be the victims of our lack of choice. But the purpose of all this is that we should have Jesus Christ's kind of dominion—that is, that we should be servants, keepers, priests in relation to the rest of creation. We are there to represent the others before their Maker and to represent to them, in our care of them, their Maker's care.

STEWARDSHIP
But we can only be the keepers and priests of the others if we are in some sense also the same as they are. And this brings us to the symbol that we have hardly named in this discussion of the relation between humanity and nature: stewardship. There is no other symbol in biblical literature that so appropriately catches the two

sides of the dialectical tension we have just been speaking about. On the one hand, the steward is singled out for a special responsibility: the steward is truly answerable for what happens in the household. All the same, the steward is one of the others—by no means superior to them, having no absolute rights over them, and is liable to judgement because of his treatment of them. The steward is different, but the steward is also the same.

There are an increasing number of ecologists, many of whom are not Christians, who find in this Judao-Christian symbol one of the most profound ways of stating the relationship between humanity and nature. Unfortunately, the stewardship symbol has been seriously trivialized by our use of it in the churches.

When we speak of stewardship as the key to the relationship between humanity and nature we are speaking of a vision. Under the conditions of history, this vision is never fully realized. It is an eschatological vision, the vision of a state of final reconciliation, in which the enmity between creature and Creator, creature and creature, creature and creation will give way to true mutuality and love: being *with*.

But while this is and remains an eschatological vision, it is not merely an ideal, an impossible dream. Today it has become the only real alternative. For to continue as nature's "lords and possessors" can only mean the end of the Experiment, for our lording over nature has become increasingly violent. There is much revenge in it. On the other hand, to adopt the solution of the Romantics and simply disappear into nature might solve the problem for the cockroaches, but what about future Mozarts? The only way is to search our hearts, our past, our present for clues as to how we might be in the world without destroying the very fragile craft that is our home. Stewardship of God's earth is no longer just a nice illusion. It has become a social and political necessity.

WATER

*For waters shall break forth in the wilderness,
 and streams in the desert;
The burning sand shall become a pool,
 and the thirsty ground springs of water...*
                    (Isaiah 35:6,7)

WATER—THE MOST ESSENTIAL RESOURCE

by Richard J. Barnet

The most essential resource of all for sustaining life is water. In large areas of the world, human beings can get by with primitive shelter and little or no clothing. A strong adult can survive for weeks without food. But without water the metabolism of the body is thrown off balance, and death comes in a matter of days. A fifth of a gallon a day is all one needs, but that need is basic in the most literal sense. Beyond the minimum needed for drinking, much larger amounts are needed for growing food, for mining metals, for producing energy, and for manufacturing anything. It takes thousands of gallons to produce a pound of beef for the table, and more than a hundred thousand gallons to make an automobile.

If we survey the contemporary world and its water needs, the relevance of Coleridge's "Water, water, everywhere, Not a drop to drink" is striking. The earth is about two-thirds water, but less than three percent of this is fresh water. Theoretically, that is more than enough. The Yangtze River alone, with a mean annual flow of a hundred and fifty cubic miles, has enough water to provide every person in the world with a hundred and fifty gallons a day. The problem, obviously, is a double one. Much of the world's fresh water is undrinkable, and that, unfortunately, includes a considerable amount used as drinking water. And then there is the problem of distribution. In many areas of the world, the trouble is too much water. In the United States, for example, it is traditional for parts of the Northeast to drown periodically while the Southwest thirsts, although in recent years Easterners have experienced both floods and water shortages. In the average year, floods take more lives than droughts.

The global maldistribution of water is even more pronounced than the maldistribution of either energy or food. The average resident of Phoenix, Arizona, which is in a relatively water-scarce area of the United States, uses, conservatively, a hundred and sixty gallons a day; an inhabitant of one of the semi-arid regions of Africa uses four-fifths of a gallon a day. The escalation in water use in the advanced countries during this century has been enormous. In 1900, the United States consumed forty billion gallons a day. Today, the figure is almost seven hundred billion. Most water for households is re-used, but, even so, because of contamination, inefficient industrial and agricultural use, and leakage in transportation, the United States loses a hundred and ten billion gallons a day. In part, the increase in population explains the heavy demand on our water resources. But the most important reason for it is that new uses for water have been found, and these are among the hallmarks of modern civilization: advanced plumbing, large-scale agricultural irrigation, and industrial cooling.

WHERE THOSE GALLONS GO

A 1962 study of water use in Akron, Ohio, by a typical family of five illustrates what has been happening in the American home. The Akron family used an average of two hundred and sixty-seven gallons a day: a hundred and thirteen gallons went to flush the family toilet; a hundred and two gallons went for bathing; fourteen gallons were drunk in various ways; sixteen and a half went for cooking and washing dishes; eleven went for laundry; three went for washing the car; and eight went to water the lawn. Typical Akron families in those days did not have swimming pools, but a pool is now an increasingly popular way to use considerable amounts of water. Dishwashers, washing machines, more vigorous toilets, the lawns of suburbia have also made water even more of an amenity in the last two decades, so the Akron figures are not extremely conservative. In many parts of the country, two hundred gallons per person is a reasonable daily average.

Plumbing, which for many people is the sole reason that they would not trade the crime, pollution, alienation, and nuclear threat of this century for any of the quieter but less fastidious ages of the past, is a devourer of water. About eighty percent of household water use is for toilets, baths, and showers.

But the biggest water user of all is agriculture. Sixty percent of the nation's water supply goes into irrigation. The process of replacing small subsistence farms with the large, highly mechanized food-producing factories — agribusiness — depends heavily on vast watering efforts.

The industrial use of water is also increasing significantly. Water use in factories has doubled since

---

Excerpts from The Lean Years, *Chapter VII: "Water: The Springs of Life." Copyright © 1980 by Richard J. Barnet. Reprinted by permission of Simon & Schuster, Inc.*

1954; however, more than ninety percent of a total of sixty billion gallons used there daily is recycled. Many modern processes require complex cooling operations. Nuclear power plants are one important example. A crucial element in a series of political setbacks for nuclear power plants in California has been the opposition of farmers, who have objected to the enormous drain on the state's scarce water supply.

As mining becomes more difficult, the consumption of water to produce energy and non-fuel minerals rises. The United States Water Resources Council, an executive agency made up of eight federal agencies, projects an increase of fifty-five percent in water "withdrawals" for mining by the year 2000. Hence the growing fights among mine operators, farmers, and environmentalists in the West. Over ninety-five billion gallons a day are used to produce energy. The Water Resources Council projects that water consumption will increase roughly ten times by the end of the century.

The deposit of wastes in rivers and streams is another form of consumption, since it renders the water unusable for other purposes. The publicizing of the death of Lake Erie and other horror stories of industrial pollution that began to appear in the early 1960's led to a continuing series of struggles over who has the right to pollute water, who has the obligation to clean it up, what is the best way to do it, and who is going to pay for it.

WATER FAMINE IN THE THIRD WORLD

The term "water famine," Representative Jim Wright noted shortly after the drought of 1965, is not hyperbole. In various parts of the world there is an acute water shortage and the availability of water is becoming an increasing source of conflict. Like other scarcities, it is most acute in the Third World. The majority of the people without sanitary drinking water live in Asia, and most of them are farmers. The World Health Organization maintains that "provision of a safe and convenient water supply is the single most important activity that could be undertaken to improve the health of people living in rural areas."

Where there is no safe well in the village — the typical situation in many regions of the third world — someone must walk for water. The fetchers of water are for the most part women and children. It is not uncommon, according to Beyer, for mothers of young children in third world countries to walk fifteen miles daily to the nearest water source. He describes a young woman he met on the road in the Sudan carrying a four-gallon tin of water on her head. Eight hours a day, she explained, was taken up with water fetching. The water system imposes its own serfdom. For many women, those are hours away from their children, away from work in the fields, or away from the chance to learn new skills. True, for some even a long walk to the well fills a social need —

a chance to stop hoeing or picking, to meet neighbors and talk.

But the fact remains that the water system in poor countries determines who will live and who will die, who will eat and who will go hungry, and how men and women — mostly women — will spend their day. The worst killers of children are the water-borne and water-related diseases that abound almost everywhere in the third world — diarrhea, malaria, and schistosomiasis, which is an enervating parasitic disease that affects over two hundred million people, mostly children. Children with worms, babies blinded by onchocerciasis, indolent boys and girls with sleeping sickness — transmitted by the tsetse fly — are part of the landscape in many third world countries. The source of all these diseases is bad water. The traditional aftermath of the floods of India is the cholera epidemic.

Compounding the public-health problem is the promotion of formula for infants by the multi-nationals in poor countries, for there the formula is often mixed with contaminated water and causes diarrhea, dehydration, malnutrition, and even death — a fact that is well known to the companies. Yet the selling of the formula in third world countries continues. The dependence of infants on the local water supply in such regions has increased dramatically. By 1974, only twelve percent of Brazilian babies were breast-fed. In the preceding generation, more than two-thirds had been on mother's milk for the first six months of life.

Children who play by open drains or stagnant pools and adults who drink contaminated water or splash in polluted streams or fish in infested ponds are doomed in the same way as victims of poisoned air. A life-supporting element has turned lethal. Sometimes the capriciousness of nature is at fault. A river spontaneously changes course and abandons those who depend on it. Or there is no rainfall. But usually water problems are created by the foolishness of humans: either they are tricked by nature into congregating in areas without adequate or decent water or they are determined to improve on nature in ways that won't work. Bangladesh provides an example of the former. Once immensely fertile because of the monsoon which floods the paddy fields for four months a year, Bangladesh became overpopulated with rice farmers. The logic of Malthus dictates that sewage deposits increase at a geometric rate, and the result is contaminated water, typhoid, dysentery, and the other water-related diseases. As for human intervention in the water system, it often makes things worse from a health standpoint. Great dams, including the famous Aswan High Dam, in Egypt, create stagnant pools, which may mean a huge increase in schistosomiasis.

WATER SHORTAGES IN NORTH AMERICA

Although few North Americans must walk miles to fill the family pail, there is a serious water shortage in the United States. In parts of the country, water is still free. It is underpriced almost everywhere. But there is not enough water to go around. From time to time, nature dramatizes that reality. There have been periodic droughts in the United States. Two or three years of above-average rainfall, according to the Water Resources Council, could relieve the shortage. That has happened in the past, but there is increasing concern among weather experts that the United States may be headed for an extended dry spell and the end of the era of cheap water.

The water problem is in large measure a consequence of our peculiar system of accounting. Because water, like air, is "free" — that is, no one owns it or the state owns it — it is used liberally in the manufacture of commodities that would be more expensive if water use were less profligate. If we ever decided that a unit of water was more valuable than a unit of money, we would presumably arrange our affairs very differently. For example, a mature steer consumes twenty-five to thirty-five pounds of alfalfa a day and drinks about twelve gallons of water. Alfalfa has a "transpiration ratio" of eight hundred; that is, it takes eight hundred pounds of water circulating through the alfalfa plant into the air to bring one pound of alfalfa to maturity. Thus, to feed the steer takes, conservatively, 2,300 gallons of water a day. Charles C. Bradley calculated in a 1962 article in *Science* that the water cost of the typical beef-rich American diet was twenty-five hundred gallons a day per person. So if we reconsider our typical Akron family of five and see them not as casual faucet turners and toilet flushers but as participants in an integrated system of water use, their consumption rate is enormous. If we rationed each person's water use in accordance with the water consumed to produce their automobile, their synthetic shirt, and their tennis racquet — and, for that matter, to print a book or a magazine — we might get more insight into the gravity of the impending water famine. But here again, prices do not accurately reflect supply and demand. Theoretically, factories pass on to the consumer what they pay for water. That is still frequently nothing, but even where municipal water charges must be paid the costs do not reflect the precious nature of the commodity or its scant supply.

THE COSTS OF INCREASING THE WATER SUPPLY

There are several strategies for increasing and improving water supplies — building dams, restructuring rivers, collecting and storing rainwater, desalinating seawater, harvesting icebergs. Each method of increasing the water supply of one city, region, or nation diverts water that could potentially be used by others; the result has been the water wars in Asia and the Middle East and the political struggles over water in this country.

Probably the most outlandish of the water-augmentation strategies is the notion of towing Antarctic icebergs to coastal deserts. The idea received considerable publicity in 1977 at the First International Conference on Iceberg Utilization, held at Iowa State University — an undertaking backed by Prince Muhammad Al Faisal of Saudi Arabia. The technical difficulties involved in transporting, wrapping, slicing and eventually melting the icebergs are staggering. But solving the water problem with the dramatic application of high technology is almost as exciting to engineers as space exploration.

Iceberg harvesting could give rise to a whole new set of military requirements. In 1978, Colonel Roy L. Thompson, of the Air Force, speculated in *Strategic Review* on the "potential for conflict" attached to the harvesting operation: "If two or more countries should be involved in harvesting within the same general area in the Antarctic, how would claims to specific icebergs be exercised and competing claims resolved?" Since seventy-seven percent of the world's fresh water is in the form of ice caps and glaciers — only half of one percent is to be found in lakes and rivers — and ninety percent of this aquatic store is at the South Pole, iceberg harvesting is an enticing technical solution. Whether, given the alternatives, it makes sense as a strategy for increasing the water supply is as yet unclear, but it is plausible enough to be a potential source of political conflict.

Desalination has been promoted as a panacea ever since 1952, when, as the geographer Gilbert F. White put it in his 1969 book *Strategies of American Water Management*, it received "sudden, almost hysterical endorsement by administrators and scientists in the United States." By 1966, about one-fifth of all United States government funds for water resources research were going to the Interior Department's Office of Saline Water. Desalination research was fashionable, and grew at a much faster rate than more important research on recycling and decontaminating fresh waste water. While desalination plants are important in the Middle East, where alternative sources are scarce, the costs of desalination are too high to make it a major solution to the water problem in the United States.

If desalination is controversial, huge public projects for managing the storage and flow of water are much more so. Dams, reservoirs, irrigation pipelines, schemes for rerouting streams, and a host of other feats of engineering are viewed by proponents—usually politicians looking for federal money, the Army Corps of Engineers, which builds the projects, and large agribusiness interests and power companies, which directly benefit from them — as modern wonders of the world. Opponents — environmentalists, Indian tribes whose land is taken or ruined, and cost-conscious politicians and bureaucrats (who usually live elsewhere) — denounce the implantation of huge concrete waterworks in the midst of America's wilderness, and the accompanying hydraulic technology, as the worst examples of pork-barrel politics and extravagant waste.

The extraordinary growth of California would have been impossible without the grand schemes for draining, pumping, and storing Colorado River water. Nonetheless, the reality remains that some of the richest agricultural land and some of the fastest-growing population centers in the United States are in a desert. Eventually, armies of engineers and acres of concrete may not be enough to sustain them.

But the era of the great water projects peaked in the 1950's, and now it is over. There is relatively little federal money for such projects today. Moreover, there is a growing constituency of dam haters. "If you are against a dam, you are for a river," says David Brower, former head of the Sierra Club and founder and chairman of Friends of the Earth, who in his career has succeeded in blocking a number of high dams.

In 1978, Cecil D. Andrus, the Interior Secretary, reported that twenty-one of the country's hundred and six water sub-regions were suffering "severe water shortages" and that by the year 2000 the number would almost double. The water table in parts of California is falling at the rate of six feet a month. (In one year, eight thousand new wells were dug in the state.) And not long ago seventy thousand wells around Lubbock, Texas — an area that produces about twenty-five percent of the nation's cotton — went dry. The water shortage is mostly concentrated in the West. The Colorado River evaporates under the hot sun at a rate of about six feet a year. Even in non-drought years, there is never enough rain. Sibley points out that west of the hundredth meridian — a line approximately bisecting the Dakotas and extending to Laredo, Texas — nearly all the land below eight thousand feet is too dry for unirrigated agriculture. West of the Rockies, it becomes desert.

SCARCITY LEADS TO CONFLICT

Because water is so obviously a finite and scarce resource, and because there are always competing drinkers, irrigators, and industrial users for any supply of water, conflict is inevitable. In the international arena, water disputes erupt periodically in bitter charges and countercharges, and sometimes in war. After the 1947 partition of the Indian subcontinent, India and Pakistan began to squabble about water. The headwaters of three

rivers that fed the rich Punjab region of Pakistan — the Ravi, the Beas, and the Sutlej — lie in India. The Cenab, and the Jhelum, which are of great importance to India, lie in Pakistan. Eventually, in 1960, with the mediation of the International Bank for Reconstruction and Development, the two countries signed the Indus Waters Treaty, which more or less settled the problem.

Israel and Syria have come to blows over rival plans to divert water from the Jordan River. South Africa justified its intervention in Angola in 1975 on the ground that it was protecting the Cunene Dam, which provided hydro-electric power for its protectorate Namibia. In retaliation for the Bay of Pigs invasion in 1961, Castro cut off the water supply to the American naval base at Guantanamo, but American technology prevailed. Desalination facilities were brought in and the base remains to this day.

The United States and Mexico have a chronic dispute over Colorado River water. As the river water flows toward the border, it naturally becomes somewhat saltier, because it picks up mineral sediments. But in recent years the diversion of considerable quantities of water for making electricity and the increased pollution of the remaining water have caused a sharp rise in the salt levels by the time it reaches Mexico. The Mexicans protested, and, after several years of negotiation, the United States agreed to desalinate part of the water flowing to Mexico, but the promise is becoming increasingly difficult to carry out. The Colorado River already serves fifteen million people, and it is sure to be drained at an ever faster rate and therefore to spread an increasing amount of salt on Mexican farmland.

Precisely the same sort of conflict exists within the territory of the United States; the conflict over water is most intense, naturally, in the Southwest. There, as in most water-short areas, the law of "prior appropriation" is in force — first come, first served. The law encourages extravagant use, since rights can be lost if the water is not used for its designated purpose. The federal government has tried to encourage changes in local law which would provide incentives to conserve rather than waste water, but reforms can be imposed by Washington only when they are attached as conditions to hydraulic bribes. In an age of austerity, there is no money for big water projects.

The convergence of a variety of political struggles encourages contradictory expectations. Nowhere is this clearer than in California. There are large amounts of water stored in the reservoirs of Northern California which are designated by contract for use in the populous Los Angeles-San Diego region. A prolonged fight has developed over plans to shoot the water south by means of a complex network of projects and waterways slated to cost about seven billion dollars. The project has been delayed because it would divert from the delta north of San Francisco water that would otherwise flow into the sea. At first blush, that might seem to be a good water-conservation measure, if a little expensive. The trouble is that the fresh water flow around the delta is necessary to maintain the ecological balance between land and sea. If the fresh water did not flow out at a certain rate, salt water would flow in and ruin the land there.

How such struggles come out will depend upon what sort of strange new political coalitions can be built around water issues. Increasingly, the costs in money and in energy of moving vast amounts of water are a public concern. The environmental damage caused by rerouting rivers, squeezing streams and building dams is becoming apparent to groups with diverse interests. The Auburn Dam, to be built on the American River in California, would destroy archeological sites in the heart of the historic Gold Rush area; the Central Arizona Project, another dam, would threaten bald eagles and other wildlife; the Meramec Park Dam in Missouri would flood caves; the Dickery-Lincoln Project in northern Maine would inundate timberland; and so on.

DEVELOPING RATIONAL WATER POLICIES

There is no adequate democratic machinery for the positive planning of resource allocation. In the absence of a coalition dedicated to designing, explaining, and carrying forward alternative programs for supplying water and energy, the victories of the environmentalists and the anti-nuclear coalitions will be short-lived. Like such military hardware as the advanced bomber and the nuclear aircraft carrier, which keep reappearing after being periodically voted down by Congress, high-technology water projects have excellent prospects for being revived. The only weapon that could perhaps prevent their recurrence is the political imagination to design a civilization that does not go on borrowing water.

Developing a rational water policy for the whole United States is not easy, if only because water is such an intensely local concern. There are two major necessities. One is conservation. Although, given the worldwide maldistribution of water, there is something more than extravagant about the use of water in the American home, the places where the most significant amounts of water can be saved are in factories and on farms. Some water specialists have calculated that industrial water use could be cut by thirty percent — most notably, by installing more efficient irrigation systems. But that would take considerable capital. Many processes that waste energy in the course of producing great heat also require considerable water for cooling. A federal commitment to the design and financing of a major industrial-conversion program is essential for saving both energy and water.

The other major necessity is regional planning. The federal government has tried unsuccessfully to promote it. There are regional planning organizations with impressive powers on paper across the country, but they do not exercise their considerable powers because competing local interests make it impossible.

The most persuasive students of water politics seem to be those who urge the return to local communities of the responsibility for providing a safe and ample water supply. The federal government cannot make local communities act in their own self-interest. If Washington gets out of the way, communities may well find that they have no alternative but to take three essential steps. One is to raise the price of water to more nearly reflect its precious nature. A second is to take public control of crucial water supplies. Private ownership of the rainfall is beyond reason. A third is for communities to get together and resolve water conflicts themselves. Such regional planning is more likely to emerge from the bottom up than by an elaborate mechanism of ukases and bribes from Washington.

"WHEN THE WELL'S DRY, WE KNOW THE WORTH OF WATER." —Benjamin Franklin

Water News from Around the World

The Face of the Waters

The earth was without form and void, and darkness was upon the face of the deep; and the Spirit of God was moving over the face of the waters.

And God said, "Let the waters bring forth swarms of living creatures..." So God created...every living creature... with which the waters swarm, according to their kinds...and God saw that it was good.

Genesis, chapter 1

And the waters flow throughout the earth, and the creation of God is baptised by the Spirit-retaining waters.

Life processes take place in a water medium. All organisms, both land and sea, are composed mostly of water, and have a watery internal environment in which the basic life processes occur.

Water is generally abundant. The planet is covered with water to such an extent that three forths of its entire area is submerged in an ocean system that connects every corner of the earth with every other corner.

Life is sustained through the continuing water cycle driven by the power of the sun. Through the power of the sun, the ocean once again offers up the water so that it can be gently laid on the petal of another flower to sustain its growth.

Of all life on the watery surface of the earth, we human beings have been the least willing to preserve the supplies of water upon which we depend to sustain us. Our ignorance and uncaring have left scars upon God's spirit-imbued water deep.

If in the complexities of our industrial history we human beings have been all too willing to afflict our water systems with every conceivable kind of waste, is there any reason to believe that we will be more careful in the atomic age?

If the life-integrating water of the earth is rendered even slightly more radioactive, then the entire fabric of life will be forever more pervasively broken, rendering the earth more susceptible to disease and decay.

All food chains which concentrate nutrients also concentrate poisons which may be present, including radioactivity. Radioactive protein means that the genetic codes for the continuation of human life will be compromised and broken, resulting in an ever-increasing incidence of cancer and genetic defects.

If we humans are not careful, we will drive the life-sustaining Spirit of God from the face of the deep. In our folly we will have created a hell on earth, the likes of which human history has never before had to confront.

Either we turn away from the nuclear demon toward the natural sources of life and energy, or the only remains of the human enterprise will be cold and lifeless artifacts of civilization clutching after the broken emptiness of time.

Excerpts from "The Face of the Waters" slideshow, National Council of Churches of Japan.

Keep the Ocean clean.
Keep Palau clean.
Keep the air clean.
Keep your hair.
Leave us alone so we can stay alive and happy.
Leave the ocean so the fish can survive and we people can survive.
Keep the nuclear waste out of the ocean.

Fifth grader
Palau, South Pacific

Marine Eco-systems Threatened

In the Caribbean, where fish comprise a significant portion of the protein intake of the people and fisheries figure prominently in their national economies, natural environmental conditions may kill off many fish, especially near the shore. The destruction of marine habitats is aggravated through the development of marinas, harbors and coastal resorts. Dams and canals also have an effect on migratory fish species and the quality of their environment.

Another major stress is pollution resulting from poor management of industrial, agricultural and urban wastes, which increase in volume as industrialization, urbanization and tourism grow. According to the U.N. Environment Program's 1982 "Regional Seas Report," less than 10 percent of the domestic waste of the Caribbean region receives treatment before disposal. One result is that several harbors are experiencing accelerated eutrophication, or the overabundance of nutrients. Oxygen deficiency is the result. Pollution from the sugar and distillery industries which dominate the economies of some of the islands has created anaerobic conditions in most of the streams and inland waters.

An additional threat to the fisheries, particularly to the coastal shrimp industry, is offshore oil drilling and the constant danger of well blowouts and accidental spills. The transporting of large amounts of toxic chemicals is yet another potential source of life-threatening pollution.

Another Dead Sea?

Writing about the Mediterranean Sea—that fabled center of the ancient world and lately, catchbasin for an exploding population's "runoff"—Rick Gore of the *National Geographic* staff says that, in spite of its reputation as "a cornucopia of sea life," its remarkably clear water actually is a sign of its paucity of life. Virtually a landlocked lake, it takes at least 80 years for the Mediterranean to turn over all its water, due in part to its depth and almost-completed enclosure (except where the eight-mile-wide Strait of Gibraltar passes between Africa and Spain).

"Whatever gets dumped into the Mediterranean stays there a long time." This includes industrial wastes and oil from commercial and pleasure craft. "Whoever eats the fish and mollusks of the Mediterranean's polluted areas is eating oil pollution," Gore quotes Colette Serruya, director of Israel's Institute of Oceanography. Also at dangerous levels, pesticides, detergents and heavy metals concoct a lifeless, poisonous ooze, which clogs river mouths and is creating a rapidly expanding dead sea.

The Mediterranean's present ill-health is the result of more than 8,000 years of human tampering with its ecosystems. And it is estimated that by the third decade of the 21st century, 400 million people will live along its coasts—not counting the seasonal tourists who invade the area. Gore leaves us wondering if, without drastic steps, the waters now gasping for life can survive such an onslaught.

Do-it-yourself Water Collecting

Women in Zimbabwe are learning how to spare themselves long, tiring treks in search of water—when it rains, at least. As part of the training they receive in women's programs of the United Methodist Church, they are taught how to construct water tanks to catch and store rainwater before it is contaminated or lost into the thirsty soil.

More complicated to build, but certainly more efficient, are the water harvesters designed to trap water in natural crevices between rocks. Once the water is caught, it is fed into three six-foot-deep pits interconnected by short pipes. The pits have been faced with bricks and stones, then lined and capped to keep them watertight and clean. Water is drawn from the center reservoir with a handpump as it is needed.

The obvious benefit of such systems is their convenience—the hours of drudgery lopped off every day. Less obvious is the growth of understanding that clean water is vital to the health of the family. An additional plus is the strengthening of the self-image of the woman who has been able to build a safe water system and then can pass along her expertise to others in the village.

Who Owns this Water?

...families on a North Dakota Indian reservation who have been without clean drinking water for years?
...South Dakota farmers who need it to grow their grain and water their cattle?
...the huge corporations studded across the Great Plains that need millions of gallons to run their industries?
...or the United States Government?

The water we're talking about is the water of the Missouri River and the underground reservoir called the Ogallala Aquifier. These two sources supply most of the

---

"Do-it-yourself Water Collecting," "Marine Eco-systems Threatened" and "Another Dead Sea" originally appeared in The Church Woman, *Vol. 49, No. 4, Winter 1983/84. Reprinted with permission.*

water to the area known as the Missouri River Basin, which includes North Dakota, South Dakota, Montana, Nebraska and Wyoming.

The problem is, this five-state region is rapidly becoming a desert. There's not enough rain, first of all. And there's been enough mismanagement of crops and grazing to encourage a desert for years. The United Nations Center on Desertification has substantiated this.

Despite the alarmingly low level of the water that remains, stripmining, coal gasification and uranium mining industries are pumping up much of it. Never mind that they contaminate much of what they use—these are profitable industries! And where do they get the water? The United States Government sells it to them.

The trouble starts when you realize that the water doesn't belong to the U.S. Government. Much of it belongs to the Indian people living on the reservations that lie over the Ogallala Aquifer or along the Missouri River. That the water belongs to these Indians should be a well-known fact to the government, which way back in 1908 guaranteed in a treaty called the Winters Doctrine that Indians on reservations would always have all the water they needed. Moreover, no less authority than the U.S. Constitution makes it clear that the government has no rights to Indian water.

But the Bureau of Indian Affairs (BIA), which represents the federal government, has been no more faithful to the Winters Doctrine than it has been to countless other treaties. For the past thirty years the BIA has cooperated with the Army Corps of Engineers as they have built dams just below Indian reservations and created reservoirs which, apart from being ecologically unsound, do not benefit Indian people at all. Moreover, the BIA has leased out huge tracts of Indian land to the ranches and corporations that are responsible for mismanaging the ever-dwindling supply and contaminating drinking water. While this goes on, Indians are being pressured to "quantify" their needs for specific amounts of water over specific lengths of time: BIA jargon for forcing Indians to agree to the theft of their water.

Who is hurting, in the end? The Indians, for one, especially those who live in isolated settlements and must frequently drive miles in pickups or even horse-drawn carts to haul back oil drums full of water that may or may not be safe to drink. The farmers, of course—they need water for their crops if they are not to become another statistic in the ever-dwindling number of family farms. Even the states are hurting as they question why the federal government is selling this water when they clearly need all the *real* water development programs they can get if their land is to remain relatively fertile. (Ironically, the mining corporations call their water-contaminating industries water "development" too.)

If all these groups that are hurting for water could see the danger of what the federal government has been doing—ever since the Carter Administration first began cooperating with the synthetic fuels industries and the Reagan Administration began actually selling water to them—they might work together to pressure Congress to put an end to it. But mobilizing people from different backgrounds is no easy feat when racism is involved. And the closer white farmers live to Indian reservations, the more racism enters into their ideas of what Indians

are asking for what they need to simply live. Thus people are kept from working together towards what could benefit them all.

What's to be Done with California's Polluted Water?

Fields of cotton and barley, orchards of peaches and oranges make California's Central Valley a vision of nature's bounty. They exist today in what used to be a desert because fifty years ago, the Federal Bureau of Reclamation undertook a huge and ambitious irrigation project to carry water from distant mountains to this valley. The trouble is, the former desert (actually, millions of years ago, an ocean bed) is still full of salts and chemicals. And a layer of hard clay deep under the surface acts like a bathtub stopper; once the fresh water gets into the soil it can't get out—it just stays there. The soil gets more and more polluted—and, ultimately, infertile.

The valley needs to be cleansed of these poisons. But how? In the early 1960's, a drainage project was begun. A canal was planned that would have carried the valley's water 200 miles away—all the way to San Francisco Bay. Sixty-five miles into its completion, environmentalists who wanted to protect the Bay (and farmers unwilling to help pay for the canal) stopped the project. The drain now empties into Kesterson Wildlife Refuge, where the water-borne poisons are wreaking havoc with the migration patterns of birds and blamed for the hatching of defective chicks.

Farmers claim they need the drain. To close it (as the California Water Resources Control Board wants the Bureau of Reclamation to do) would mean that farming would cease on some 42 thousand acres of prime farmland. The only other way to stop the pollution would be to limit the amount of water entering the valley. Yet the area's economy depends on water "imported" from the mountains.

When it Comes to Clean-up, the Water Belongs to Everyone

All over the world, complex scenarios like the one described above are being played out. Sometimes, as with California's polluted fields, there are so many separate interests that no solution gains enough support to go full-steam ahead. But polluted water is everyone's business. In the article that follows, Louisville Courier-Journal *reporter Larry Tye describes how, both in Europe and in the United States, water clean-up works best when there is regional cooperation—when "everyone with a stake in the problem is involved."*

America has transformed the Ohio River and dozens of other waterways from free-flowing sewers to fish-filled rivers over the past several decades. But things are at an impasse: The rivers aren't as clean as they should be, and the federal government, which is drafting a new clean-water bill, is running low on commitment — and money — to finish the job.

For the Ohio, this means that problems with storm sewage, agricultural runoff, toxic chemicals and other hard-to-get-at pollutants will probably persist. Its waters may never be clean enough for safe swimming and other recreation.

Water experts on the Ohio and other waterways agree that America needs a fresh approach to the cleanup, one that won't bust the budget. They think the pollution-fighting experiences of West Germany's Ruhr River and Britain's Thames River may provide just the approach they're after.

The Germans developed an unusual scheme: They brought all the industries and cities along the Ruhr together to administer — and pay for — cleaning up the river.

The Thames program was equally effective: One of Europe's dirtiest rivers was turned into one of its cleanest. And it was done at bargain rates.

The Ruhr faces problems as imposing as any river anywhere. Ten percent of Germany's 61 million people and 40 percent of its industries reside in the Ruhr Valley. Coal mines, steel and textile mills, and chemical and paper plants — all heavy polluters — line its banks.

Yet the Ruhr must supply drinking water to 70 percent of the valley and just under 10 percent of the nation. That is an imposing demand upon a river just 141 miles long — one-seventh the span of the Ohio.

The Germans long ago responded to these special challenges with a special program: In 1913 they created two utility-like agencies, one to fight pollution and the other to ensure adequate drinking supplies.

The cleanup group runs the 118 wastewater treatment plants, 20 miles of interceptor sewers, five low-level dams, 61 pumping stations and five power plants along the Ruhr. The supply group operates five large and nine small reservoirs, five major hydroelectric plants, along with other systems involved in storing and selling drinking water.

Membership in the agencies is unique, by American standards. The cleanup group includes all communities and industries discharging anywhere in the valley; the supply group involves anyone using the river for drinking water or electricity.

This means that everyone with a stake in the problem is involved. And it ensures that one group, with the power to act anywhere along the river, holds actual cleanup duties.

In the United States, responsibility for cleaning up waterways is shared by federal, state, local and regional agencies. This often leads to confusion, frustration and expensive duplication of effort.

The Ohio offers a case in point: Four federal, one regional, eight state and hundreds of local agencies are all fighting river pollution. Some groups don't pull their weight; others lack authority to rigorously pursue cleanup efforts. As a result, the cleanup is often stalled or stopped.

American water cleanup bureaucracies also leave out industries and other parties whose help is needed to eliminate pollution. This breeds an adversarial relationship between industry and government: Industries clean only what they're made to, and government must fight for even this marginal progress.

The payment scheme for the Ruhr River programs is also unusual: Polluters are taxed based on the amount and danger of their effluents, with fees set steeply enough to discourage continued pollution. Groups using the water to drink, produce energy, or for any other purpose are taxed based on how much they use. This ensures that polluters, and people who benefit from clean water, help pay for the cleanup. With costs borne by local groups, there is more incentive to economize.

To pay for sewage-treatment plants and other capital projects, the pollution-control agency can issue bonds. It can also apply for federal grants to cover up to 50 percent of the costs.

This approach contrasts with water-pollution programs in the United States, where the federal government has paid up to 75 percent of the costs of sewage-treatment plants and shares other water cleanup and enforcement expenses. Under the U.S. system, sewage-treatment projects have cost more than needed, and money was often spent on projects that failed.

The Ruhr approach has been tried in the United States — in the Houston area — and it's considered a stunning success.

In 1970, the Gulf Coast Waste Disposal Authority took over water supply and cleanup responsibilities from several communities and industries near Houston. It runs 20 municipal sewage-treatment plants serving 120,000 people, along with four industrial facilities serving 42 industries. More cities and firms are joining all the time.

The reason, deputy general manager Joe Taylor says, is that the authority has proved it can "treat waste in larger volumes at a lower cost than small plants." Well-trained operators at the authority's large plants do a better job than small-town sewage officials, who may double as public works directors or dog catchers.

"We primarily learned that regionalization pays, that you've got to treat a water system as an entire unit," he said. "What we do up at this end of the river affects what happens down there."

The British have also learned that the approach to cleaning up water helps determine its effectiveness — and its cost.

Before 1974, British water officials faced many of the same difficulties their U.S. counterparts face today: persistent pollution, splintering of responsibilities and poor planning in the use of dwindling financial resources.

The Water Act of 1973 changed that. It consolidated 1,600 sewer agencies and 187 water-supply groups into 10 regional authorities. The Thames River Authority, for example, handles pollution-control, navigation and water-supply activities for 12.1 million people living along Britain's best-known and grandest river.

After monitoring the British system for a decade, Daniel Okun, a University of North Carolina professor and water resources specialist, concluded it is revolutionary and could prove of great use in the United States. He said regional systems:

- *Fight pollution more efficiently.*

The U.S. sewage-treatment program is in a perpetual state of crisis: Small communities often can't effectively operate sophisticated sewage-treatment plants: large ones have their own problems. Each city is preoccupied with solving its problem, losing sight of the overall river cleanup.

In spills in Britain, a regional authority would issue a warning to all its plants, and the response would be uniform. With larger, regional treatment plants, each facility would have the sophisticated technology to respond to toxic chemical spills.

- *Handle water shortages better.*

America has about 50,000 small water systems, each depending on its own source and 99 percent serving fewer than 50,000 people. Most can't afford technical or financial expertise needed to plan for emergencies, so during dry spells they often run out of water.

"Regionalization works so well because the authority, which runs the water works for all these communities, knows the options, has better management and can quickly straighten things out," Okun said. "And systems can be connected with pipelines so that all towns won't run out during an emergency."

- *Are more economical.*

Britain has shown that fewer people are needed to do the job, be it water supply or pollution control, when dozens of small agencies are replaced by one large one.

Copyright © 1984. The Courier-Journal. *Reprinted with permission.*

LAND

The land shall not be sold in perpetuity, for the land is mine; for you are strangers and sojourners with me.
(Leviticus 25:23)

LAND, PEOPLE, CHANGE

What can we learn from traditional societies
about the relationship between land and people?

by B. David Williams

"We will not realize how much we have to learn from them until we discover how much we ourselves have lost."

While there is no turning back history, it could be very clarifying to think about the radical transformation that has taken place in modern times in the relationship between people and the land. For so-called "traditional" agrarian societies, stability, balance, harmony and solidarity were over-riding values. The ground was not just a place on which to live and produce. It was the seat of cultural ties, the focal point for human relationships — and, for some, it was the perceived place of biological and spiritual origins. The idea of "using" the land in the western sense, the thought of wearing it out, probably never occurred to these traditional communities. Community leaders were given the power to allocate limited rights for the use of land. Those who were present had access to land, while those absent had more limited access. Because of the nature of tools, transport and communication, one person or family could exploit only a limited area. In the tropical world, subsistence crops grew more or less continuously and were not well-suited for storage and transport. Economies were based on trading, rather than cash, which tended to limit the accumulation of wealth. Provision was made to make food available to those in special need or unable to grow their own food.

Modern societies tend to be models of continual change and mobility. High value is placed on individual freedoms. The accumulation of property by individuals is invariably a part of the success model, even when many in the community (even within the family) are quite poor economically. Land is perceived primarily as a place on which to live, a resource for production, an investment, a location from which to do business. It is valued for its usefulness in production or for its speculative value. Land rights are often absolute—and within the bounds of zoning ordinances there is little restraint on the right to exploit or transfer ownership of the land.

We can read about this "modern" reality even in the Old Testament! As early as the eighth century, B.C., the prophet Amos preached passionately to the people of the Northern Kingdom of Israel about the abuses being experienced by the poor as the rich got richer (Amos 5:7-13; 8:4-6). This was a time of prosperity—and great religious piety! It appears that farmers, particularly small landowners, were especially victimized. Their land and other property were taken in foreclosure by urban entrepreneurial families. A large new economic class was emerging: landless rural people who worked the vineyards and farms of their increasingly rich overlords.

Throughout history, when lands were colonized, they invariably inherited the land laws and land use practices of the colonizers. This led to the concentration of landownership among a few people and to absentee ownership. Agricultural lands became more important than forage lands, since its products could be stored and/or sent away. So forage lands diminished. The development of tools, transport and communication, along with introduction of money economies and new kinds of land ownership laws gave individuals effective "rights" and control over the development of land.

The money economies provided unusual, exciting opportunity for the consolidation of wealth and power by those with capital, vision and skill. The demand for storable, transportable agricultural products burgeoned with the growth of urban centers. Eventually, structures of enterprise and control were formed which made it possible to use land and food to control large populations of people.

Even today, as traditional structures collapse, large numbers of people are losing the security of their traditional economies; they cannot relate effectively to the larger, cash-oriented economy. The problem is found in modern societies, too, where huge agro-business enterprises, structured for efficiency only in relation to the economic goals of the owners, and responsive to ill-conceived agricultural policies, gradually take over

---

B. David Williams is a United Methodist missionary who has served in the Philippines, Papua New Guinea and Fiji. He is currently on loan to the Asia and Pacific offices of the National Council of Churches of Christ in the U.S.A. as Associate Director for Peace Issues.

more and more land—and more and more people are left out of work.

So the poor, especially the rural poor, are left out of rapidly growing "modern" economic sectors. Strangely, the late 20th century U.S. family farm fits this pattern. From 1978 to 1982, largely due to economic pressures, the number of U.S. farms of 50 to 999 acres decreased by 111,750—an average of nearly 28,000 farms per year. The number of Black farmers decreased by 11 percent, Hispanic farmers by nearly 9 percent during the same period.

Unfortunately, only a few countries—invariably those experiencing *severe* land shortage—have enacted effective basic reform. This has taken place through purposeful, peaceful change to support important social and humanitarian values. What should land reform mean for societies considering themselves to be modern and progressive? Traditional societies may have some important lessons and values to share with us. After visiting the Tasaday, the so-called "lost tribe" of Mindanao, Philippines, in 1969, a Filipino anthropologist told me, "We will not realize how much we have to learn from them until we discover how much we ourselves have lost."

THIS LAND IS HOME TO US

by David Liden

The Appalachian Land Ownership Study was unprecedented in several ways. First, there were no consultants flown in to do a simple survey; Appalachian people "owned" the study from beginning to end. Nor did their findings gather dust on the shelves of Washington policymakers; instead, they spawned new projects and reenforced work already begun.

The people who designed the research methods and gathered the statistics were teachers, farmers, students, church people, lawyers, housewives and unemployed people. They started out knowing that something was wrong with the way a lot of their neighbors lived and they suspected that it had to do with who owned the land they lived on. So for two years they worked together interviewing local people, gathering and coding countless points of information, sampling patterns of land ownership and property taxes across six states and eighty counties. They investigated the impact of absentee and corporate land ownership and discovered why some of the most devastating poverty in the United States is found amidst some of its most valuable real estate.

While the Appalachian Land Study deals with only one geographic region, its conclusions can be translated into the contexts of other regions of North America, wherever people—landowners, tenants, investors,

farmers—are trying to be responsible stewards of the land. In the following article, Dr. David Liden, who coordinated the land ownership study in West Virginia, reflects on Appalachian reality.

"What the rest of us have occasionally seen through a glass darkly, we can now see spelled out with unmistakable and irrefutable clarity." That's what John Edgerton in *The Progressive* said about the Appalachian Land Ownership Study. Let me give you a sense of what that picture is.

We recorded data on over 10,000 land holdings comprising over 20 million acres in 80 counties. We found that corporations, government agencies and absentee landholders, along with 1 percent of the local population, owned at least 53 percent of the total surface land in the 80 counties. In eight counties, four of them in West Virginia, corporations owned over one-half of the surface land. In eleven counties, eight of them in West Virginia, corporations owned one-half of the minerals. In McDowell County, corporate interests owned 76 percent of the surface land and over 100 percent of the minerals. Over 100 percent? It's possible because you have layered coal that can be independently owned and then you have oil and gas layered *under* the coal, so you have different kinds of minerals that can be independently owned. They're listed separately in the tax books. When you add them up, you get over 100 percent, relative to the surface.

We found gross under-assessment of this corporate/absentee owned property, especially the mineral property. Over 75 percent of the mineral owners paid less than 25 cents an acre in property taxes. In the major

---

Dr. Liden is director of Rural Resources and coordinator of the Western North Carolina Alliance. He and his family live in Murphy, NC. This article is adapted from a presentation Dr. Liden made at a 1983 consultation of the Coalition for Appalachian Ministry. It originally appeared in ERETZ: land—The Church and Appalachian Land Issues, ©Coalition for Appalachian Ministry, and is used here with permission.

coal counties, the average tax per ton of coal reserves was only one-fiftieth of a cent. The worst cases were from Kentucky, where the average property tax per acre for minerals was only one-fifth of a cent! As a result, the total property tax received for mineral property, for 12 counties where some of the most valuable coal in the country is found, was a mere $1500 in 1979. N & W Railroad, which owns over 80,000 acres of coal in Martin County, Kentucky, paid only $76 in property tax. In West Virginia, the state which is doing the best job in the region in terms of taxing coal, the most valuable coal is going untaxed.

Additional research has addressed the under-assessment of oil and gas reserves and the lack of any kind of adequate tax on the production of oil and gas. For instance, in West Virginia, oil is worth an average of $30 to $40 a barrel; it's valued at 56 cents a barrel and the tax rate is applied to the 56 cents. Commercial timber is going untaxed in most Appalachian states. The North Carolina timber lobby recently won tax exemption for their commercial timber stands. Commercial timber is not taxed at all in West Virginia.

So, in a word, if you can put in a word, the Appalachian Land Ownership Study explains why we have some of the most devastating need amidst some of the most valuable land in the country.

HOW CORPORATE CONTROL OF LAND AFFECTS PEOPLE'S LIVES

It's no longer possible to explain away the problems of the region with simplistic stereotypes such as the character of the people or with the common rationalization that somehow the Appalachian region was bypassed by the economic mainstream. The Appalachian Land Ownership Study shows that Appalachia is very much a part of the economic mainstream and always has been, yet in a very colonialistic relationship. What does it all mean? I think a West Virginia farmer who was part of the study summed it up best. He said, "Some way, somewhere back, we lost ourselves. I think it was when the companies bought up the land."

What the impact of absentee/corporate control is, it is clear to us now, is not just control over land, but more importantly, it's control over jobs, over housing, over the local power structure itself. What we concluded is that as a result of this kind of captive influence the conventional redistributive and participatory mechanisms are simply not working in Appalachia. The interests which own and control the wealth of the region are not bound to return their fair share to local communities. And the nature of their control precludes any real involvement by local communities in how the land is owned or used or in making decisions about the quality of their lives.

Let me describe the relationships between large-scale, absentee commercial ownership and the quality of life. The relationship with education is clear enough once you realize that 80 percent of the property tax goes to the school system in most of the counties we looked at. Once you document that time after time, county after county, an equitable tax simply isn't there, you can understand the condition of the schools throughout rural Appalachia.

The housing situation shouldn't surprise you either. In many cases, land is simply not available for housing. In Logan County, West Virginia, we interviewed Chamber of Commerce people who said that there simply was no place to build another house in Logan County. The companies own all that's left. That explains why you see trailer after trailer on rented company slabs. You might be a miner earning a fairly decent income, but you can't apply that income to a home for your family because the land simply isn't there.

Other results of this kind of land control include population decline, job loss and community instability, as well as the decline of farming as a way of life. Since the middle 60's, over a million acres of Appalachian land has been taken out of agricultural production: a loss of over 17,000 farmers, or 26 percent of the farming population.

The relationship between absentee land ownership and the political structure was in many ways most interesting of all because of its subtlety. What we found through interviewing was that large commercial interests that own land in the community hold a very definite degree of influence over the behavior of local political people. We found conscientious county officials who'd say, "It's bad, I know it's bad, I sure wish I could do something about it," but who were simply intimidated by the prospect of a corporate lawyer coming to their office, saying they had no right to do this or that, using

23

jargon, threatening lawsuits and treating them like bumpkins. So county officials may be with you in spirit many times, but they're paralyzed when it comes to doing anything about it. In some cases, local officials are starting to emulate the secretive, paternalistic style of the corporations themselves. That means they don't share information at the school board meetings, they don't share information at the county commissioner's meetings, they don't share information with the county newspaper. They better represent the interests of the corporate landowners than those of their own community.

THE LESSONS ARE IN THE LAND

I think what we're seeing in Appalachia is part of an inherent contradiction in the direction of our national life itself. Certainly the fate of the land is central to all our concerns—social, economic, political and spiritual. We're seeing an aggregation of capital in this country like we've never seen before. We're seeing a centralization of decision-making like we've never seen before. We're seeing collusion between economic and political power. On the other side, the opportunity structure, especially in rural areas, is being closed off. The demise of the family farm and farming as a way of life reflects the demise of small enterprises in general. The declining power of organized labor, the attack on environmental quality and the narrowing of the realm of political alternatives are other examples.

So it's a systematic problem. What we have to do is start thinking of some responses, some alternatives to this trend. I really believe, in sitting and thinking and reflecting, that there are lessons, necessities built into the land itself. I've started calling them "imperatives."

First of all, land holds a *biological* imperative as to what it can do best. When this is violated, the land dies. We are now learning that extended application of certain chemicals, heavy equipment and heavy tilling will retard and destroy the land's capacity to nurture and sustain.

There are also *economic* imperatives in the land. There is growing evidence that small and medium-scale enterprises are more innovative, more productive, more secure and more satisfying than huge corporate structures. A similar cost/benefit assessment on developing and reclaiming mountaintop strip-mining shows that the costs far outweigh the economic advantage of having that coal. There's also a very good argument that points out that non-structural alternatives to flood-control are much more economical than the huge projects proposed by the Army Corps of Engineers, even without factoring in the human costs of lost farmland.

I think there's also a *spiritual* imperative in the land. I suggest that if we study traditional cultures and listen to these people, we'll begin to understand that if we let it, land can teach, provide solace and nurture, and introduce us to humbling mysteries.

Then there are *political* imperatives that are lodged in the land itself:

1. Look at the history of a lot of the corporate ownership in the mountains. The land study acquainted us with a powerful oral history arguing that much of this land was taken in a fraudulent, deceptive manner in the first place. We heard story after story of mineral land taken from unsuspecting landowners who "sold their minerals for pennies," having no conception of their real value or the potential destruction in the development of that mineral. Secondly, there was the use of "quit-claim" deeds, where people who had no right to sell sold land to corporate agents. They had no authority to sell it because they didn't own it! The use of ancient, expired land grants or patents was another tactic. A woman told me about the agents coming around to the farms and to her home. A stranger showed up one day—they welcomed him, he stayed for two days and scoped out the situation. Then he came back a month or so later with documentation that this particular farm, which had been in her family forever, in fact belonged to his company.

2. It's also important to recognize that there are limitations on the ownership of property in our own tradition. Historically, the state is an embodiment of the commonweal and is authorized to expropriate private land for the general good. This is an affirmation that the community's claim to land is prior to and higher than the individual's claim. Unfortunately, eminent domain has not been used in a very effective way; it tends to be used on behalf of power companies, railroads, construction companies and the like, rather than on behalf of the local community. As a result, it doesn't have a lot of credibility. But the concept is there. There *is* legal and historical foundation for policy affirming the public's right to land.

Let me refer briefly to our own political traditions: the Lockean tradition and Jeffersonian tradition. The natural right theory, which meant the "inalienable right" to life, liberty and property, for John Locke, and to life, liberty and pursuit of happiness, for Jefferson, is really a philosophy of limits. Locke went to great lengths to explain that while he believed in the inalienable rights to life, liberty and property, there were definite limits on the amount of property a person or interest had a claim to. The limit depended upon how much a person could use in a reasonable and worthwhile way. Land, for Jefferson, was a key component of political power. The concentration of land ownership, said Jefferson, will result in the similar concentration of political power. Economic democracy was possible only if people had the opportunity to protect their well-being, or happiness, and land was central to that well-being.

Liberal political theorists have always recognized that Locke and Jefferson were talking about conflict between the right to land and the responsibilities that go with that land. These are conflicts, they say, which should be resolved in the political marketplace. In fact, they are not. The Land Ownership Study is full of examples of corporations defending their vested interests in the political marketplace with trained lobbyists, political campaign financing, batteries of lawyers and access to the media. Community people also have vested interests, obviously. But they don't have the means; they don't have the resources. Their vested interests are usually less focused, less articulated. They presume that their elected and appointed officials are the ones who are representing their interests in that marketplace. But "who gets," in the political marketplace, is really determined by how these issues are framed and how resources are allocated.

For example, some public TV people in West Virginia did an hour-long documentary on the land study. They spent a day in my front yard; they interviewed my neighbors and talked to me and we outlined the problem. Then the little van full of TV equipment went down the road, and I thought, "Oh my gosh! Whatever happens, happens!" Then they talked to all the company people: N & W Railway, Columbia Gas, Island Creek Coal, and they had us. It wasn't at all a fair situation. We lined out the problem and the companies replied, but we never had a chance to come back and say, "Well what they said is full of hot air." *We* never had a chance to reply. For example, one of the executives from N & W said, "Well, Dr. Liden is talking about the public's right to land, or access to land. Yet here we are — the largest landowner in the county. As I understand my American history, that's the kind of democracy I know, we've got an exclusive right to this land because we bought it." I never had a chance to say, "Let's put that to a vote in McDowell County!" So whose definition of democracy are we talking about?

3. I want to explore the idea of corporations' right to land. The way land is referred to now is part of what I call "secularization of the mountaintop." Land is referred to in very instrumental ways: "residual property," "marginal property," "raw property," "waste land." We're creating a whole vocabulary that denudes and despiritualizes the land so that we can then come in and do with it as we please. The U.S. Capital Corporation is constructing a ten-story condominium at the top of Little Sugar Mountain in western North Carolina which will be visible from three states. The condos are going for about $100,000 a unit. And the president of the corporation justifies this development by saying, "Every rich person deserves a mountaintop." So the "mountaintop" has become a means to an end: whether it be the view, the exclusiveness of it, its coal, or increasingly, now, for the federal government, a way of balancing the budget. All of this is creating a spiritual void. I think it's our responsibility to fill that void, to start creating some new language and concepts and myths about land.

KEEPING THE LAND FOR THE PEOPLE

There certainly is a role for the church in all of this. We have to come to terms with the motives behind the exaggerated ownership that we're seeing in our own experience, our own time and our own place. In order to work towards this, we should explore and support ways of influencing and controlling the land by influencing and controlling (1) the value of that land, (2) the use of that land, and (3) the supply of that land.

The *Wall Street Journal* has said that land is one of the best speculative commodities — better than diamonds. You have guaranteed infinite demand and a limited supply. Capital is running to the land for that very reason. And if we can influence the value of the land, we can intervene in this speculative craziness. There are a number of ways of controlling the value of land. Zoning, for instance. When you zone an area residential, you restrict its value. You can restrict subdivisions. You can create something like a transfer-tax so that every time land is bought or sold, a substantial tax is put on the transaction. Contributing or selling developmental rights is one technique for farmland preservation. Or you could think about "registering" the value of the land, freeze it as a "real value" point or create a "real value" in terms of the land's value for homes, food and sustenance.

The result of these kinds of strategies would be that land would be available to a younger generation which, at this point, can't buy land in Cherokee County, North Carolina, where I live. Farming would continue as a profitable enterprise. The argument that agribusiness can grow cheaper than anyone else belies the hidden subsidies, the interstate highway system, for instance, or the federal support for all kinds of chemical research and the hidden cost in the fact that land is being destroyed by those businesses in the process of growing food.

There's a lot of land in the Appalachian region that was bought not just for speculation, but because it has valuable natural resources as well. Is there any way of controlling the *use* of that land which would influence its value? Stiffer environmental regulations could control it, certainly. There's almost no control on oil and gas development in the Applachian states, for instance, some on the timber development, more on coal mining, obviously. Stiffer environmental controls are going to influence the value of that land. Now they're talking about a ridge law in western North Carolina—ten-story condos can no longer be built on mountaintops. There is also talk about deleting areas from mineral development for environmental reasons.

Tighter or more expensive condemnation procedures can also influence how available land is for alternative uses. You might be familiar with the Stonewall Jackson Dam struggle in West Virginia or the Brumley Gap struggle in Virginia or the Randleman Dam proposal in North Carolina. These are all examples of attempts to condemn some of the best agricultural land in the region for dam projects. The value of that land at condemnation time is typically determined by the government—and then by the courts if that value is challenged. What if the people who were going to lose their farms determined the value of that land? I think this would be an effective way to control how land is used. It would simply be too expensive to proceed with dams which, in the case of those mentioned above, are marginal benefit at best!

We can also influence who owns the land by controlling the supply. Subdivision restrictions are an example of this: for example, someone can no longer chop up 40 acres into 160 homesites. You can tighten the septic requirements or the water requirements. You can do a lot of things that seem logical and reasonable but simply aren't being done in a lot of areas today!

Family Farm Acts in the Midwest prohibit the acquisition of family farmlands by corporate interests. Why not pass Family Farm Acts in Appalachia? There are also various kinds of incorporated areas in the United States. I think as church people we can start thinking along these lines. I don't think we have to get bogged down by the attitude that, "Well, we've got all these great ideas, but how do we ever enforce them?" It's not the church's job to enforce them. But I think it's the church's job to exert moral authority *and* moral example. The church needs to go on record with its vested interests. The mechanics can come later.

I want to issue a challenge: Why not take a look at your church's investment portfolio? Insurance companies own over 800 million acres. Most of it is prime farmland. Where are your pension plans and retirement benefits coming from? On the question of church land: What are you doing with it? How much of it is tax-exempt? What does this do to your county's tax base and ability to provide services?

Take a look at the numerous land struggles going on in your region. Investigate where they come from. Get to know the people involved. Within the struggles for land are the bits and pieces of the vision that we're all looking for.

WHERE HAVE ALL THE BLACK FARMERS GONE?
by Joseph F. Brooks

Historically, the Black community in America has been closely attached to the land. The vast majority of the slaves brought to this country worked either directly as field laborers or in some domestic capacity on a Southern plantation or farm. After Emancipation, the freedmen necessarily remained largely in land-based pursuits, usually agreeing to some sort of tenancy or sharecropping arrangement with white landowners.

When slavery was outlawed in the U.S., it was clear that two needs had to be met if Blacks were to survive as a people: they had to be educated, and they had to acquire land. Agriculture was the primary industry of the country, and Blacks saw their survival directly related to their ability to become successful and prosperous farmers—and to own the land they farmed.

By 1910—the peak year of Black landownership in the U.S.—in the face of hostility and violence, Blacks had managed to own in full or in part more than 15 million acres.

But by 1940, that 15 million acres had dwindled to 12 million, and roughly 210,000 Black farm operators had disappeared. Thirty-eight years later, the 1978 census of agriculture revealed that the number of Black farm operators had been reduced to a mere 57,000 with control of, or access to, only 4.7 million acres. At this rate of decline, there soon will be no Black farmers left to count.

The factors that have pushed Blacks off the land and out of the rural South are varied and complex. One of the major initial factors was the mechanization of cotton. The Black farmer was unable to remain competitive because he lacked the capital to purchase the new

Joseph Brooks is president of the Emergency Land Fund, 564 Lee St., SW, Atlanta, GA 30310. From an article titled, "The Loss of Black-owned Land in America," excerpted with permission from ruralamerica, *published 6 times yearly by Rural America, 1302 18th St., N.W., Washington, DC 20036.*

mechanical harvesting equipment, and his plot was too small to warrant using the new techniques.

These difficulties, added to those from which he already suffered—his inability to obtain credit on reasonable terms because of his race, poverty or both; the racial discrimination to which he was subjected by government agricultural agencies; and the general bias against small farmers that still permeates many government farm programs today—combined to push him off the land. And the same Southern traditions that handicapped Blacks in acquiring an education also prevented them from acquiring experience in business, marketing and finance.

Other factors—including the migration of Blacks to urban areas in search of better-paying jobs, the continuous erosion of the family farm, misguided government agricultural policies, the emphasis on capital-intensive farming and others—have contributed directly to the removal of Blacks from agriculture.

Concentration of landownership in America has taken on a different meaning in the 1980s. In the 1950s and '60s, U.S. industry was importing raw materials from developing nations, converting them to finished goods and selling them back to the same developing countries. Since then, the terms of trade between the U.S. and the third world have changed. These nations now are dictating the price of their raw materials, causing dramatic shifts in U.S. industry. The emphasis now is on the development of the indigenous resources of our own countryside.

Accordingly, there is a rush for land to supply the minerals, food and other vital resources we previously imported. Some have suggested that for the U.S. to become self-sufficient in energy alone, some 55 million acres beyond what is currently available would be needed.

This industrial demand for land—coupled with cheap labor, the need for housing and an ever-expanding agribusiness industry—has put the small landowning farmer in an extremely vulnerable position. The situation for the Black landowner is compounded in the Southeast, given its tradition of racism and discrimination.

The irony of all this is that Black farmers do as well or better than their white counterparts on a gross-return-per-acre basis. The net farm and farm-related income earned by Black farmers per dollar value of land and buildings is almost 15 percent, while the average net return for all farmers in the U.S. is 9 percent.

THE EMERGENCY LAND FUND

The Atlanta-based Emergency Land Fund (ELF) is an effort to help individual Black farmers and other rural landowners retain their land. ELF has concentrated its work primarily in the Southeast, but over the years it increasingly has been assisting Blacks outside the region who have a down-South interest in rural land.

ELF is seeking out these "uncounted" Black landowners—more than half of whom, or some 740,000 individuals, live outside the South—and educating them about how to retain their land despite often clouded titles. Typically, this land is occupied or owned by poor elderly people who cannot read or write—making it particularly vulnerable to tax, partition and foreclosure sales and easy prey for land speculators.

ELF is now organizing in Chicago and elsewhere outside the South. October 29, 1984 was proclaimed "Chicago ELF Day" by Mayor Harold Washington and an overflow crowd attended an ELF-sponsored "Up South" land forum and reception at Chicago's St. Mark's United Methodist Church. There now is a steering committee in place in Chicago that includes several attorneys and 30 volunteers who are assisting with ELF's efforts in the area.

Clearly, what we need is a national policy that offers viable options for landownership. The importance of owning land cannot be measured by economic criteria alone: landownership should be viewed as a vehicle for

human development as well as economic development.

Studies have indicated that landowning Blacks are more likely than non-landowners to register and to vote, to participate in civil-rights actions and to run for office. In effect, landownership in the rural South confers on Blacks a measure of independence, security and dignity that is crucial to elevating the status of the Black community.

Serious attention needs to be paid to the political, social and psychological consequences of Black land loss. The stake that the Black community feels in the United States as a nation—and their sense of belonging and security—may very well hinge on whether they own any significant portion of the national territory and have roots in the land. The nomadic experience of the Jewish people may have something to suggest in this regard.

It is the Black farmer who has suffered the greatest displacement as a result of the modernization of agriculture. The need for equity and the incorporation of human values into our agricultural system grows more apparent with time. The question is, is time running out?

DOMINATING THE LAND
Land News from Around the World

Sacred Land Controversies

Indian nations contain some of the richest uranium, coal, oil and other strategic resources on the continent. Government agencies have not been shy about acquiring or leasing this land to the energy industry. Commercial development, mining minerals, constructing tourist facilities, diverting waterways—makes it impossible for Native people to exercise the "sophisticated balance between the physical and the spiritual landscape that is the will of the Great Spirit" and deprives Native Americans of the right to "freely exercise traditional religions whose spiritual center is the land." So writes Anita Parlow in a statement from the Sacred Land Project of the Christic Institute in Washington, D.C.

"The Elders say that subjecting tribal people to uranium waste dumps, ecological havoc, deformed births is an unacceptable sacrifice to the dominant culture's excesses. Traditional Native Americans offer alternative values—a land-centered dynamic worldview...an awareness that centralization, control and the illusion of indefinite growth will destroy not only traditional religions but possibly the entire planet."

Native people involved in sacred land controversies across North America can benefit from the support of the churches in their efforts to vindicate their first amendment rights, Ms. Parlow concludes.

For information on sacred land controversies, contact either the Indian Law Resource Center, 601 E. Street, S.E. Washington, D.C. 20003. (202) 547-2800; or the International Indian Treaty Council, 777 U.N. Plaza, New York, NY 10003.

"Terminated" Peoples

In 1954, the federal government conducted experiments to "Americanize" native Americans in Oregon. The Klamath and Western Termination Acts stated federal condemnation of Indian reservations and the severance of tribal ties with the U.S. Government. Unstated was the assumption that terminated tribe members would move into non-Indian communities and adopt American "apple pie" culture and lifestyles. The "sink or swim" hypothesis upon which the experiments are based has profoundly affected the lives of sixty-four Oregon tribes.

Absolutely nothing was done to prepare the people for this transition. Tribes and their members were simply cast aside, their economic base wiped out, their land base sold, a whole new set of state laws imposed, including taxation of lands. The people were suddenly bereft of tribal institutions and the educational and health benefits available to all other recognized Indians. Most difficult of all was being told they were no longer Indians.

Among the affected were the Confederated Tribes of Grand Ronde Indians, whose once-magnificent reservation consisted of one million forested acres. Termination has caused the confederacy, consisting of over sixteen tribes and bands, economic and social devastation. Reservation lands were sold to non-Indians and each tribal member given $24.80 as total payment.

The Cow Creek Band of the Umpqua Indians were

"The Devastated Hills," "Disappearing Rain Forests," "Terminated Peoples" and "Uprooting Third World Farmers" are excerpted with permission from The Church Woman, *Vol. 49, No. 3, Fall, 1983.*

never recognized as a tribe because they refused to join a forced march in 1856 (in which over half of the participants died) and fled into the hills. However in order to survive, they have had to come out of hiding and blend into a "foreign" culture.

The traditional land of the Coos, Lower Umpqua and Siuslaw Indian tribes is on the south-central coast of Oregon. Removal to a reservation took them away from this homeland, but when the reservation was opened to white settlement, they had to return to their ancestral lands—where they live now with no land of their own.

The struggle of Native North Americans to lay claim to ancestral land has been long and painfully disappointing. Occasionally, however, a bright spot appears on the horizon to revive hope that it hasn't all been in vain. Such a case was the recent decision by a U.S. court of appeals in response to a Native American couple's defense against eviction by the Bureau of Land Management. The grounds were that the ranch they had operated for many years constituted trespass on public range land. The decision announced that the title of approximately one-fifth of the state of Nevada actually belongs to the Western Shoshone tribe, the original owners, because no public land laws were ever passed to extinguish this claim! Moreover, no money for the use of this land was ever paid by the federal government to the Shoshones.

"The decision shows that there is some justice for Indians in the U.S. court system," said Jerry Millett, chairman of the Western Shoshone Land Federation, noting that while millions of acres of land are affected by the decision, the Shoshones have no desire to threaten private property interests. "Our struggle is with the U.S. Government, not our fellow Nevadans."

The Devastated Hills

The Himalayas. What romantic images they evoke. Crystalline peaks and rushing water at the roof of the world. Mile after mile of fir and cedar. Breathtaking vistas and hardy people untouched by Western culture.

This is the romance, but unfortunately not the reality of the Himalayas today. As Rashmi De Roy reports in the New Dehli/Bombay *Times of India,* their exploitation in recent years has been so rapid and destructive that ecological degradation threatens almost the entire range. It is feared that Nepal will be denuded of its forests by the end of the century.

The picture De Roy draws is ugly and shocking, one of increasing desertification driving the hill people down from the mountainsides. Silt carried off in the ground water to discolor the Bay of Bengal for four hundred miles offshore creates new land masses in the river channels and chokes trout by clogging their gills. It is a picture of vital springs drying up and ecosystems destroyed by the uncontrolled exploitation of timber and other resources. The habitats of bears, snow leopards and Kashmir stags are being wiped out.

De Roy tells us that over twelve years, forests have been diminished by almost 12,500 acres, and the process continues. In some areas, dense vegetation has been reduced to scraggly patches of fifty acres or less. As trees are timbered off, the exposed ground becomes infested with weeds and other useless growth. Or it erodes, leached of its potential for rejuvenation and creating the perfect setup for avalanches and landslides. The removal of the natural organic "litter" on the forest floor has reduced the small-animal population and the number of seeds that could renew the forest. Experts estimate that it will take years of non-interference by humans and grazing animals to restore the decimated timberlands.

All this due to the insensitive headlong rush into development, misnamed "progress": orchards and croplands illegally encroaching on the forest land; the invasion of wood-based industries and a tourist business calling for more and more wood and a spreading network of roads to service it. De Roy concludes his article: "Conservation forestry is imperative if the Himalayas are to remain habitable."

The tragedy striking this beautiful and proud mountain range may be half a world away and remote from our lives. Yet it is as close as the forests in our own land that are being sacrificed for much the same reasons and with the same devastating results. The Himalayas cannot wait any longer for help. Neither can any other mountains whose forests are disappearing.

Disappearing Rain Forests

Vanishing at an even more alarming rate are the tropical forests which, biologically, are the world's richest land areas and host to half of all living species. Lloyd Timberlake, writing as editorial director of *Earthscan,* tells us that almost half of them have already been lost. The remainder are being disrupted at the rate of one hundred acres a minute. Is it possible to conceive of six thousand acres of forest disappearing in an hour? In a single day, 144 thousand acres?

As the forests disappear, so does the rich variety of plants, animals and birds. Whole species are wiped out when these species are found only in this one particular place. Fresh water sources, flood and erosion management, climatic patterns and fuel supplies also are seriously affected.

We can only imagine what this is doing to the forest-dwelling people of Latin America, Africa, Southwest Asia and Oceania, where the moist tropical forests are found. Timberlake reminds us that "as the jungles go, so go the tribal people who live in them"—drastically reduced in number as their ancestral lands are taken for development. Brazil's Indian population of six to nine million in 1500, for example, is less than 200 thousand today—an attrition rate of two million per century. And these are people who live in special harmony with the jungle forests and treat them with the utmost respect.

One tragic aspect of the extermination of forest peoples—whether through death, the inability to replace themselves or forced assimilation into the dominant society—is the tendency to regard them as nuisances. "Nomads are considered difficult to organize, administer and tax," Timberlake points out. "Collective land ownership is a foreign concept to most governments." He cites atrocities committed in order to get land or as the result of exaggerated fears of the ferocity of tribal peoples or the belief that they are subhuman. Tribes have been bombed from the air with dynamite or murdered with food that was laced with arsenic. "Once deprived of their land, forest dwellers can only look forward to absorption into the lowest level of the dominant culture as beggars, landless peasants or low-paid laborers."

The major cause of jungle destruction is industrial development, with profit as the motive. Timber harvesting for building materials, paper products or fuel, or to provide acreage for agriculture and ranching accounts for the largest percentage of the timbered-off land. Many politicians and planners consider forest growth of little economic value beyond the wood it produces and the space that its removal provides. They do not count of much consequence the life that it supports.

Because of this narrow, self-serving vision of those pushing the jungles to extinction and the power they hold, the outlook for saving the forests is dim. However, steps are being taken on a world scale to study the implications and brighten that outlook. Satellite monitoring, radar and aerial photography supplement the ground surveys being taken by some of the jungle-supporting countries. Data from U.S. satellites has helped the U.N. construct a country-by-country picture of forest cover and the rate at which it is disappearing. UNESCO's "Man and the Biosphere" program is combatting widespread ignorance about forest ecology. Alternative sites for agricultural and settlement projects are being sought.

What happens in one part of the world ultimately affects every other part. There is no living alone or for ourselves any longer. If jungle lands and their people, animals and plant life are to survive, the support of all concerned persons is necessary.

Land

Doomed to eternal torture
  I cannot bear it any longer
To see you scalped and raped
  by earthlings and non-entities
See how they lacerate you
  and incapacitate you
Violate your person and
Suck life out of you
Yet you suffer in silence
  the indignity of castration
    total annihilation
And gradual descent into nothingness.

But your plea becomes crystal clear
  Your conditions are simple
  You don't want a concrete forest
  Infested with subhumans with the
  Noose around their necks.
You want to bargain life with life
You have a fertile womb
  Ever ready for the act of procreation
Adam was your offspring
But has divine sanction
    to commit incest
      till you enfold him once again
  in the embrace of death
    while in transit.

Sitiveni Ratuvili

From Christian Rural Mission in the 1980's: A Call to the Liberation and Development of Peoples: *Report on the Rural Mission Consultation, Jayuya, Puerto Rico. April, 1979. Used with permission. Sitiveni Ratuvili is a rural pastor in Fiji, South Pacific, and participated in the consultation.*

Uprooting Third World Farmers

A great deal of the violence, tyranny and uprooting that is taking place in "underdeveloped" countries in Latin America, Africa and Asia centers around the disruption of land rights in the growing of cash crops. Some situations are comparable to the transformations of the classic European feudal systems, wherein the peasants worked the land and contributed a portion of their produce to an "overlord," who, in turn, provided security against intruders and settled local disputes. Goods were also allotted to the religious leader of the community, who provided spiritual and ceremonial services. The peasants had the right to retain a portion of the produce for their own use, or at least had access to communal land where they could farm or graze animals.

The expectation in this type of society was that every member of the community would have enough resources to carry on the collective struggle for survival. The systems were dismantled during the 17th century in England, the 18th century in revolutionary France and in the 19th century in Germany. Along with the resulting instability came opportunities to become workers in the new factories or to migrate to the "New World."

In the 20th century, the pattern of uprooting rural people is greatly complicated by the fact that there is little or no industry in many countries to absorb the dispossessed. Anthropologist Eric Wolf has noted that, paradoxically, "it is the very attempt of the peasant to remain traditional that makes him revolutionary." Examples of bitter struggles abound: in Mexico, where traditional Indian lands were taken over by hacienda owners; in Algeria, where the French seizure of lands disrupted the balance between pastoral and settled populations; the decay and collapse of the public granaries in China, which contributed to the breakdown in that society.

CULTIVATING THE EARTH

*Thou dost cause the grass to grow for the cattle,
and plants for people to cultivate,
that they may bring forth food
from the earth...* (Psalm 104:14)

A LETTER TO THE CHURCHES ON THE CRISIS IN THE AMERICAN COUNTRYSIDE

by David L. Ostendorf

July, 1984

My dear friends:

Greetings and peace from the American Heartland!

The summer of 1984 has given us record June rainfall and flooding, but we rejoice in the fact that most of the Heartland is experiencing more normal weather patterns as the summer winds down.

But again this year, the lush countryside is deceiving, and easily masks the pain and suffering of the people of the land. Our own workload this summer is a clear reflection of the seriousness of the rural crisis. Organizing meetings have continued without let-up across the state; farm families are still being sold out in frightening numbers; organized farm protests are slowly becoming more accepted by the people of the countryside; our Farm Survival Hotline is still ringing; and more demands are being placed on our staff for training clergy, mental health professionals, attorneys and others in dealing effectively with the human, legal and financial "fallout" from the growing crisis in agriculture.

We had hoped—as recently as last winter—that the peak of the crisis had been reached, and that the number of farm operators forced off the land would begin to decrease. We were wrong; the peak may be another two years or more away. With ever-mounting debt loads, low commodity prices, increasing interest rates, declining land prices, and government that is turning its back on the crisis after throwing billions of dollars at it in the 1983 PIK program that—once again—provided substantial benefits to large, well-off corporate "farms," small and medium-size family farm operations face a grim, uphill battle for survival.

In our major public report in 1982, appropriately entitled "Crisis in Iowa Agriculture," we predicted a "tidal wave" of farm losses if the agricultural economy did not improve. By early 1984, "farm crisis" had become a commonly-used term by media and concerned politicians throughout the region; in the spring of 1984, government and university reports indicated that we faced deep and lasting problems in rural America.

On March 28, 1984, for example, the Iowa Department of Agriculture issued the results of its Farm Credit Survey, taken among 2500 farmers and 230 leaders across the state:

- 5 percent of Iowa's farmers "are in such serious trouble that they may be forced out of business in 1984";
- another 5 percent of the state's farmers "are carrying such heavy debt load that they may be out of farming in 1984 or 1985";
- "about 40 percent of our farmers are carrying a debt load beyond the average which probably means they can not survive long-range";
- "total farm debt in the state has climbed to $17.5 billion and farmers who are in debt cannot carry that load at current high interest rates and returns from farming which are currently only 2.3 percent of the assets invested."

The Iowa Secretary of Agriculture—after several years of denying there was any particular problem in the countryside—also said publicly upon release of the Survey that: "If 10 percent of our farmers leave the land, we are talking about the loss of about 11,000 farms and a farm population loss of nearly 60,000 people. Should this happen, it would be a staggering blow to Iowa where eight out of 10 jobs depend on agriculture and the rest of the economy is also troubled."

The farm crisis, of course, extends well beyond Iowa and the Heartland, and other data underscore the seriousness of the crisis throughout the land:

- Net farm income in the U.S. dropped in 1983 to its lowest level (nationally) since 1971; preliminary USDA estimates as of early July, 1984, indicate that it will stand at a level between $15 and $17 billion.
- Nationally, the delinquency rate for loan repayments to the Farmers Home Administration (FmHA) by its farm borrowers stands almost 4 points above the same period last year,
- Nationally, the Production Credit Association (PCA), a major farm lender, has dropped from 384,000

David Ostendorf, a United Church of Christ minister, is director of Prairiefire Rural Action, an action and advocacy organization based in Des Moines, Iowa. He has coordinated the American Farm Crisis Project since 1982. "A Letter to the Churches" was written as a report to the National Network on Town and Country Ministries of the United Methodist Church and presented at the meeting of its leadership gathered in England during the summer of 1984. It is excerpted with permission.

active farm borrowers at the end of 1982 to less than 341,000 at the end of 1983—a decline of 11.2 percent. Many PCA farmers face extraordinary legal and financial problems with the Associations they borrow from. Several Associations across the country have gone broke; others have consolidated their operations.

- Farm debt in the U.S. has climbed to some $216 billion, with about 25 percent of that amount held by people who will be unable to make the next two years' interest payments on it. Farm debt is getting ever-larger, and is being concentrated among operators heading for insolvency.
- Comparing debt to net farm income, it is clear that medium-size farms are in the most serious trouble. On average, debt for those farms with sales over $200,000 annually is less than 4 times their annual net farm income, while debt for farms with sales of $40,000–100,000 annually is 23 times greater than net farm income.

When we look at the plight of minority farmers and landowners, the situation is even worse. Rural America's Research Director, Dr. George Rucker, recently completed an analysis of the Census of Agriculture and found that: In the South, which accounts for 3/4 of all non-white farmers and 95 percent of all Black farmers, the decline in minority farmers between 1974 and 1978 was more than four times as great as for white farmers—13 percent compared with 3 percent—and continued to fall by another full 10 percent between 1978 and 1982. [See "Where Have All the Black Farmers Gone?" page 26]

The data and statistics and analyses, of course, can go on and on without ever mentioning the human cost of the crisis, or without ever raising the more fundamental issues we face economically, socially and politically as a result of the crisis. I'd like to share some reflections in this regard...

It has been my privilege—and our organization's privilege—these past two and a half years to work with, organize, support and minister with farm and rural families throughout the nation's Heartland. We have, in that process, worked with literally thousands of farm families who face the imminent threat of financial collapse and the loss of the only livelihood they have known.

In that process, they have coped with the disparaging remarks and judgments of government officials, lenders, other farmers, and even chuch leaders, who fall into that classic American trap of "blaming the victim" for their own problems. Up until early this year, it was not unusual to hear from public officials that those farmers in trouble were simply the "poor managers," the "over-extended," or those who probably shouldn't be in farming anyway. "We are removing the inefficient..."

These are callous words from people who are responsible for helping bring about this crisis in the first place—from people who have little experience with its human toll. It is a toll measured in the tearful eyes of men and women—from their twenties to their seventies—who see no way out from the pressures of their financial situation. It is a toll measured in the agony of people who have done "everything right" during their farming careers, and who may even have had their farm paid for in full at one time, only to lose it during the '80's. It is a toll measured in the frantic call to the Hotline that a farmer has just left with his rifle for the bank to settle the score with a lender who will no longer go along with him. It is a toll measured in farm suicides: the father of seven, in his forties, a farmer all his life, under extreme financial pressure, despondent and hopeless, who went to the barn and shot himself in the head. It is a toll measured in health problems that people have never experienced before; in stress that tears apart families; in increased abuse of substances, spouses, families; in accidents resulting from carelessness. It is a toll measured in the frustration of a farmer forced off the land, and trying for months to get a decent job in town or city, where there are few jobs available in the first place. It is a toll measured in the faces of parents who are barely able to keep food on the table or who can't pay the bill to heat their farm house. It is a toll measured in the tones of pastors and other leaders who talk of their communities dying and going through the grief process as an entire community. It is a toll measured in the low voice of a small-town businessperson who announces that his doors are being shut because farmers aren't buying his goods. It is a toll measured in the unemployment lines of Waterloo, where workers who build tractors and farm implements are laid off because farmers can no longer afford new equipment.

Still—and we hear this often—there are farmers who "have never had it so good." This is certainly true: those who carry little or no debt load; those who own their land, and who simply tighten their belt a little more these days; those who may have escaped the vagaries of the weather and bad crop years.

For us, this points to the most disturbing aspect of the current farm crisis: its displacement of more and more people from an ever-shrinking pool of family farm owner-operators, and its reinforcement of the steady movement toward a two-tiered structure of agriculture in which fewer, larger and more highly-capitalized farms produce more of our food supply, while medium-sized farms are eradicated or forced to rely heavily on off-farm income to survive.

In short, we may not be all that far removed from the "Central Americanization" of the American Heartland.

For at the very heart of the current crisis in American agriculture, there glares a disturbing moral and political issue: Who will control the land?

Church leaders from all over this nation are making the journey to Central America to see and hear the story of oppressed and landless people, and to witness the struggles for freedom that are so deeply rooted in the peoples' understanding of their faith born anew of liberation theology. Some of those same leaders, however, cannot find the time to make the shorter journey into the nearby countryside to see the suffering among their own people of the land, or to witness how the land is being lost and concentrated in their own midst, and the people displaced from it. I have thought seriously of late about starting some Central America tours of my own for these travellers—tours of Central America, USA.

It is not, of course, the physical journey that prevents us from seeing and understanding what is happening in our own nation. It is, I believe, the psychological and political journey that keeps us so distant and removed from our own people of the land. We still hear of "hicks" and "hayseeds." The stereotypes of farmers, rural business people, rural pastors, working people and other professionals are often derogatory, and sometimes scathing. The people who feed us are depicted as rough, crude and not too bright, or they're depicted as shrewd, cunning and greedy four-wheel drive, air-condition- and stereo-soaked tractor jockeys out to plow up America.

But it is perhaps the political journey into rural America that is most difficult for us to make, for it is a journey that may threaten some of our most fundamental and deep-rooted beliefs about "how America works." It is this very journey, in fact, that has jarred so many of our rural people into action these past several years, and that has prompted them to call into question the institutions and structures of society that even they have taken for granted... and that have failed them when they needed help most.

Quite bluntly, that political journey is also one that disrupts our own churchly status quo. It is difficult for a local pastor to have to confront the conflict standing between the farmers and the bankers in the pews on Sunday morning. Indeed, while we often draw eloquently on our Judeo-Christian heritage for guidance on stewardship and on just distribution and use of the land, we also sanction by our silence the consolidation of control over the land, and the displacement of farm and rural families from it. We give the notion of family farming lip-service, and lean upon the Jeffersonian ideal of "small landowners being the most precious part of the state," while virtually all our farm policies and programs breed bigness, consolidation of control over the land and capital-intensive, industrialized agriculture. We countersign rather than counteract...

The implications of this process for democratic government are worth pondering. In the long run, those who control land also control people. One does not have to make the journey to Central America to see that happen. The displacement of Native Americans to reservations; the loss of over nine million acres of land by Black Americans in this century; the colonial status of Appalachia and other resource-rich areas of this country—all underscore the grim truth about the relation of controlled land to controlled people.

Land is the most basic social property of any society; even though it may rightly be owned by individuals, its use, control and preservation for the whole of society and succeeding generations are the responsibility of all people and of those democratic institutions that represent them. It is also the responsibility of the people of the community of faith.

"We are left to see if it is possible for us to embrace solidarity with the dispossessed..." wrote theologian Walter Brueggemann in his book, *The Land*. This indeed is the challenge before us as the church in the midst of the current crisis in the American countryside. It is a challenge we take on because we affirm the most fundamental biblical understanding of land as a gift, a trust, a covenant from God, and not simply as property to be bought, sold, or liquidated. The land belongs to God, we read in Leviticus, and we are but strangers and guests upon it. The land, the prophets tell us throughout the Old Testament, is avenged by the God who gave it in covenant. "Woe to those who...add field to field, until there is no more room, and you are made to dwell alone in the midst of the land," Isaiah cries out. "Woe to those who devise wickedness...because it is in the power of their hands... They covet fields and seize them; and houses, and take them away; they oppress a man and his house, a man and his inheritance," Micah warns.

"To embrace solidarity with the dispossessed..." We

are called to take a stand. We're going to "bend some people out of shape" and incur the wrath of some institutions if we're honest about doing it. We're going to make some enemies. But the church has done that before; it survived and even grew stronger in the process.

Over the past year, we have made good headway in our tasks. We celebrate the "quantum leaps" made in organizing and empowering the people of the countryside! We celebrate their new voice on the American political scene. We celebrate the extraordinary support and ministry provided by the dispossessed to one another...and to those with possessions. We celebrate the emerging vision of community, and all the acts of community-building in the countryside. We celebrate the larger church's support and solidarity, and its willingness and commitment to heed the call to justice from the people of the land.

"To embrace solidarity with the dispossessed..." We must not let up now. The next several years will be critical to the very survival of family farm agriculture in this nation, and to the health and vitality of all rural America. We must continually strengthen our pastoral, prophetic and political work in the countryside and in the centers of power.

Let me provide some suggestions for action in all these areas of work—the pastoral, the prophetic, and the political—and I think you'll begin to see the opportunities we do have before us to embrace solidarity with the dispossessed of the American countryside:

—We need to train and prepare pastors and lay leaders in ministries to farm and rural families in distress. That training should include counselling techniques; a basic understanding of the crisis, its causes and its symptoms as manifested in individuals and families and communities; dealing with community conflict; knowing where to turn for help with financial and legal problems being faced by those families; and encouraging people to join together in confronting the broader, common problems that have caused the crisis in the first place.

—We need to do a far better job in preparing pastors for rural ministry in our seminaries. The church, like other institutions of the society, has difficulty legitimizing rural work/rural ministry...and it shows. Rural ministry is often viewed as an apprenticeship before "real" ministry is available in the bigger churches of the suburbs or cities. Salary levels reflect that view in most cases, as do notions of "career advancement." We need to reverse this! We can do so by offering more, stronger seminary courses that prepare people biblically and theologically for ministry with the people of the land; courses that provide macro-economic training so rural pastors have a better sense of the economic forces and realities of contemporary rural and farm life; pastoral counselling courses that focus specifically on ministering with rural people, their special needs in time of crisis, and their pride, independence and isolation that often makes it difficult for them to come forward and seek help; courses that deal forthrightly with issues of social and economic justice in our own land.

—We need to educate all our people—rural, urban, suburban—about the importance of family farm agriculture to this nation and the world, and about the relationship between food production, distribution, availability and cost. This in itself is a massive undertaking, for it requires that we attempt to bridge major cultural gaps in our own society. It means helping the person who has never been in the countryside understand the importance of the land and its people to the survival of the city. It means helping people who have never thought that the grocery store shelves could be empty, or the price of food skyrocket if its production and distribution were controlled by a few interests, understand that the farm crisis of the '80's could be the food crisis of the '90's. It means teaching and re-enforcing values and perspectives on economic and social justice that only the church can bring to so many at once.

—We need to bridge the remaining gap between paper and practice, between what our churches have so eloquently said and written about family farming, rural life and the land and what our churches have *done* about those concerns. Church doors can be opened up to meetings; leaders within the church can be identified who will participate and lead efforts to bring people together. The church can be active in coalitions of diverse groups that are growing across the nation in response to the crisis in the countryside.

—We need to look prophetically at the way the church uses its own land and money resources. What is our institutional responsibility with regard to the land we are given or that we now control? When that land is sold, whom do we sell it to: a young, beginning farmer at a price and financing level that would enable that farmer to get a good start? Or to the highest bidder? Why can't we invest our massive investment funds in rural banks that are willing to work with farmers during this period of crisis, and develop loan packages for farmers with our funds at lower-than-market rates in cooperation with those banks? As an institutional investor, our record in this area is not good. A church in southern Iowa has been working well over a year now to get a commitment of $100,000 from a related national agency in New York—money that would be invested in a CD in a local bank and used to help farmers. They have encountered unimaginable paper work and red tape. At one point, they thought everything was in place, only to find out that they had to go back with more information, forms and paper work. To this day, not a dollar has been committed to that rural bank, to those local church people who tried so hard to use church investment funds in this creative manner.

—We need to activate or strengthen in every conceivable way the churches' work in the public policy arena on farm and rural issues. The churches' policy analysts and lobbyists in the state capitals and in Washington must listen to and work with their people at the grassroots. The institutional church—individually and ecumenically—must hear and heed the dispossessed as it moves to change public policies and make government accountable. We need to think about creative new ways to lend our voice to the development of the 1985 Farm Bill, so as to assure that it does not become another patchwork quilt made by special interests to the exclusion of the long-range interests of family farm agriculture. We need to help guide and develop a long-term farm and food policy for this nation into the twenty-first century.

—We need to begin thinking about how the church can facilitate international discussions on trade and development as it relates to farm and food policy in this nation. What would happen if we in the church were to develop linkages between church/farm leaders in the U.S., other developed nations and the Third World nations? What if we were to sponsor an international forum on farm and food and land policies? What if we were to develop linkages between the peoples of the land, as we have developed linkages between the peace movements of the global community?

—We need to identify potential political leaders in our midst, and encourage people to run for public office, regardless of party affiliation. We need to help get out the vote all across rural America...and we need to do solid educational work to help those voters cast ballots for those who would bring justice to the people of the land.

The struggle ahead for the church in rural America will not be an easy one. As I think about what that struggle means, I only have to recall what has happened over the course of 24 hours this week alone. After taking a number of "routine" calls at the office one afternoon—Hotline calls from farmers facing lenders' pressures, calls related to an upcoming farm protest, calls to finalize farm meeting arrangements—I came home for supper and an evening with visiting family members. About 9 p.m., I got an urgent call from a farmer friend alerting me to the possibility that the sheriff would be rounding up his cattle. He was seeking help in spreading the word so our farmers might be ready to show up at his place on short notice to support him if that happened. A half-hour later, another close farmer-friend called to talk at length about his bankruptcy and an upcoming inventory check on his farm that he did not want to permit; he was tense, angry and on the edge. The next morning, I picked up the paper only to read a letter to the editor from a farmer angry about a penny auction we were recently involved in. Later, I got a call from a reporter friend who had just learned that a 45-year old farmer active in the Farm Unity Coalition had died suddenly that morning from a heart attack. As his priest said, the hard work and stress had taken its toll. That same afternoon, a 44-year-old broke, displaced farmer came in the office looking for help. He was having a hard time finding a job in Des Moines, but had been working at a restaurant occasionally, and walked some seven miles to work, because his car had broken down.

There are thousands of stories across rural America like those from this one day...

"To embrace solidarity with the dispossessed..." We must act. For to be silent and passive these days is to abandon and dismiss the people with whom we work and live and depend on in rural America—the people who seek to live on the land and who provide food and resources that sustain the society. To be silent and passive these days is to abandon and dismiss a religious heritage that has sustained, nourished and inspired generations of people who believe that God acts—and continues to act—in history, in the struggle for justice, even against heavy odds. To be silent and passive these days is indeed to ignore those among us who are dispossessed, who are losing their livelihood; who are threatened with the loss of their land; and with the loss of land, the loss of an economic base and the demise of democratic institutions.

We must put faith and hope into action and works of justice with the people of the countryside. We must be bold and prophetic; liberating and reconciling; strong and courageous. We must be builders of a world of justice...justice for the people of the land and the countryside, and justice for all the people of all the nations.

We must, indeed, "embrace solidarity with the dispossessed," so we can look back upon these days of crisis, and affirm with joy and thanksgiving that we did not refuse the responsibilities given us or shirk the opportunities before us to make the broken whole, to set at liberty those who are oppressed; to minister with and empower the dispossessed, and to build creatively a world where justice prevails on the land and among its peoples.

Grace and peace to you...

David L. Ostendorf

FARMING, BENSON-STYLE

by Bob Shoemake

The glaciers that covered the North American continent at the end of the last ice age were good to the United States. They leveled the Great Plains and left them the most fertile land on the planet, an enormous prairie covered by a layer of topsoil one and a half to two feet thick. One part of this prairie, in the southwest corner of Minnesota just two miles from the Iowa state line, is a very special farm.

Since 1939, members of the Benson family have been caring for, and been cared for by these 160 acres of God's good earth. On March 1 of that year, Gus Benson, a Swedish immigrant, and his wife Bertha, a Finnish immigrant, moved from Nebraska to their new farm in Minnesota. There, until their "retirement" in 1968, they worked the land, tended the animals and reared a family of three daughters and a son. In 1971, David, their son, and his wife Sally, having spent most of the '60's fighting the draft and working in California, moved back to the farm to learn from Gus and Bertha and to take their turn as stewards of this land.

I first visited "the farm" during Thanksgiving weekend of 1982. Drawn by people I have come to know and love, by the land and by a vision of life which resonates with my own, I have returned many times. During my visits I have helped with most phases of the farm's work, from hoeing thistles and making hay in the summer to spreading manure and shearing sheep in the winter.

Gus and Bertha still live in the farmhouse, helping with the chores and giving advice, support and love to David, Sally and their kids. Gus is 81 and often works outside, milking Blomma (Swedish for "flower") twice a day by hand. Though he has a weak leg that makes it hard for him to walk, with his barrel chest and arms the size of saplings he can pitch manure or dig post holes for hours without tiring. Bertha just turned 75. Her easy laugh and marvelous baking provide a warm welcome to the farm's many visitors.

In the 13 years since they came to the farm, David and Sally's family has grown to include a daughter and a son. Through years of working, they have refined and clarified their vision of what they are building at the farm. Sally, Massachusetts born and bred, has become a feisty "farm woman," learning how to butcher, garden, can, spin, weave, make soap and cheese, drive a tractor and more. At the same time she works as director of a Montessori school in the nearby town of Worthington. David farms with a confidence and skill learned from his father and from years of experience. Nights and some winter days, he also works as a mechanic, maintaining the farm's ancient machinery and the cars, trucks and tractors of friends and neighbors. On a shelf in his garage is a television tuned to the public channel. (Sally says that people can endure almost any kind of isolation if they have access to public radio and television.) Many nights, while rebuilding an engine or fixing a car, we have watched the tube with one eye and talked about the farm.

Agriculture, for David and Sally as for Gus and Bertha before them, is conceived and experienced relationally. Relationships between God and the created universe, between the planet and its inhabitants, between people and their food, between land and animals, between technology and production, between "culture and agriculture" and between families, friends and neighbors are all important to farming. Says David, "Each farm should be a unit in which the social, economic, ecological and spiritual are synthesized," and each unit is interdependent with all other units. We must care for the land, say David and Sally, because we have a relationship with it; it provides sustenance for our lives.

Their vision of agriculture leads the Bensons to farm in a way that seems increasingly uncommon among American farmers, that is, working a small, highly diversified, family farm using "clean" methods and moderate technology.

In the middle of January, when I last visited the farm, its fields were covered with a thick winter blanket of snow. Because it is located on an erosion-prone hillside, special measures are necessary to ensure the farm's continuing fertility. In addition to contour plowing and cultivating, one of these measures is *not* plowing in the fall, leaving the crop stubble to catch the snow and hold the soil. (The snow-free fields of many other farms and the black snow that fills their road ditches attest to the dangers of fall plowing.) When spring comes, these fields will produce wheat, rye, oats, corn, alfalfa, soybeans and birdsfoot trefoil for pasture.

Reprinted with permission from Alternatives, *Vol. 10, No. 1, Spring, 1984.*

Instead of trusting nitrogen fertilizers with their concomitant health risks (many of the wells in Nobles county are polluted by nitrates, a common problem in the Mid-West), the Bensons depend on other means to nourish the farm's soil. In addition to rotating crops and using "green manure" (nitrogen-fixing legumes like alfalfa and soybeans), an important component of soil nurturance comes from farm animals. David says that even if he didn't eat meat, which he does, he would keep animals for the role they play in maintaining the soil. The farm menagerie includes stock cattle, sheep, steers, geese, dogs, cats, and a milk cow and horses. This spring, chickens and perhaps a hog will be added.

Of all the animals, David's pride and joy are four black Percheron draught horses, enormous beasts that stand taller than a car. Gus farmed with horses until they were displaced by tractors in the '40's and '50's and David remembered and loved them from his childhood. When he began to farm, he bought a team—Mollie and Nellie—and Gus taught him how to work with them. They are used primarily for spreading animal manure and raking hay. Using the horses allows David to spread manure in the winter without fear of getting stuck in the snow. It also spares the land soil compression problems caused by the use of heavy tractors. The Bensons do use farm machinery: combine, swather, tractor, corn picker and so on; however, to avoid the large size, fuel consumption and cost of much new machinery, they use older, lighter equipment, often modified by David to increase efficiency.

A big weed problem for Midwestern farmers is the Canadian thistle. Many farmers rely on an extremely potent and dangerous herbicide to control these weeds; David and Sally rely on crop rotation and their friends and family. Each summer, a number of these folk come to the farm for a week or more of thistle hoeing. Early mornings and late afternoons are spent walking the rows of beans and corn and the oats field hoeing the thistles; the rest of the days are spent swimming in one of the farm's three ponds, cooking, eating, sleeping or helping with other farm chores, thus nourishing relationships with both the land and the other people who are working. In exchange for this work, David keeps the family's fleet of aging Volvos running.

Farming Benson-style is very labor-intensive, but this hard work is not disdained. "I like the connection that exists between working with my body and the food that I eat," says David. Jobs like thistle-hoeing or hay-making that demand many people are accomplished with the help of neighbors, friends and family. Rarely does money change hands in these encounters; instead, labor is traded for goods and services are bartered.

The farm is not a big moneymaker. Most years it supports Gus and Bertha and provides a third to one half of David and Sally's income. The rest comes from David's shop and Sally's teaching. Sally, especially, feels ambivalent about this arrangement. While she enjoys the challenge and social stimulation of teaching, she has less time for cheese-making, spinning, weaving and the other things for which she came to the farm. A shortage of cash also slows progress on the earth-bermed, solar-heated house they are building on the farm place and means that they must continue to commute from the old farm house a half-mile away.

The production of income-generating agricultural commodities is one measure of a farm's fertility. Its production of food, friendships and other relationships is another. Most of the Benson's food is home-grown. Animal products include milk, cream, butter, cheese, beef, mutton, lamb and goose as well as wool for spinning and weaving and down for insulation. Wheat and rye yield flour while from the garden come berries, fruits and vegetables. The animals are pasture-fed throughout the spring, summer and fall. In the winter they eat home-grown corn and alfalfa. Soybeans and oats, both difficult to process at home, are sold, often for seed.

While chores are a year-round constant of farm life, they vary with the seasons. In the spring, summer and fall, the land demands long hours of attention; winter turns the focus to the animals, the machinery and dreaming about the future. Sally yearns for the completion of the new house and the time and work it will save, time she could spend creating with her hands — cheese, knitted and woven goods. David thinks about the possibilities of having a Percheron stud for breeding, of adding some more dairy cows, of developing a cheese plant and of the "world car," a versatile, easily-repairable, intermediate technology vehicle that could sensibly be used in the developing and developed countries of the world. Both think about the changes that will come when Gus and Bertha die. They are working now with David's sisters to develop a strategy so that the farm can be maintained intact.

Farming is an art based on the nurture and balance of relationships. As they reflect on their family's art, all of the Bensons remember their teachers and look forward to the coming generations of artists.

PESTICIDES—A GLOBAL AFFAIR

They may be illegal to use in North America, but harmful pesticides still lace a lot of the food we import from developing countries. How did those pesticides get there? Read on...

Tasty but Toxic

by David Weir

When government import inspectors in Dallas opened up a shipment of cabbages from Mexico not long ago, they smelled insecticide. As is routine, the officials took a sample for laboratory analysis and let the rest continue on to market. Then the verdict came in. The cabbages contained illegal levels of BHC, a pesticide severely restricted in the United States because it causes cancer, birth defects, genetic mutations and other reproductive disorders in test animals, even in very low concentrations.

By the time the Dallas inspectors received news of the contamination, the cabbages were in supermarkets, refrigerators—and stomachs. No alert was issued. Except for an obscure reference in a government report

---

David Weir is a senior staff writer at the Center for Investigative Reporting in Oakland, CA. He has researched and written extensively on pesticide issues and is co-author of Circle of Poison *(1981). This article is excerpted with permission from* The Dial Magazine, *October, 1981.*

sometime later, the public had no way of knowing the incident had occurred.

In Santa Clara County, south of San Francisco, Marta Rojas, once a chemist in an electronics firm, hesitates to walk past the fruit and vegetable counter in supermarkets. In her work, she had been excessively exposed to chemicals and now suffers from what her doctor has diagnosed as "immune disregulation." Whenever Rojas comes into contact with a new chemical, for instance, pesticide residues on fresh produce, she feels an allergic reaction coming on and soon after breaks out in welts and rashes and has difficulty breathing.

There is a connection between the cabbage shipment and the chronic suffering of Marta Rojas, and it involves the negligence of the U.S. government in protecting its citizens from harmful chemicals, particularly pesticides. The government's own surveys show that 25 percent of all the pesticides on the market can cause cancer. The surveys also show that many of these poisons find their way into our food due to a loophole in the major law governing pesticides, the Federal Insecticide, Fungicide, and Rodenticide Act (FIFRA). Through it, companies can continue to make any pesticide for export, even after it is banned here.

BHC (the compound in the cabbages from Mexico) used to be manufactured by the Hooker Chemical Company (of Love Canal fame) for both export and domestic use. In 1976, the company voluntarily removed a purified form of the pesticide from the U.S. market because of a dwindling demand for it. Hooker officials claim they no longer make it for export. Nevertheless, dozens of chemical companies do manufacture pesticides that are illegal or restricted here and export them to third world countries.

The reason American consumers are directly threatened by this regulatory failure is that our food supply system is a global affair; we import over $17 billion worth of food products a year. Based on spot checks of very small product samples, the Food and Drug Administration (FDA) has estimated that at least 6.9 percent of these imports are contaminated with illegal levels of pesticides. Our technology, then, comes full circle, ending up on our dinner plates.

The General Accounting Office (GAO), the investigative arm of Congress, attempting to figure out the problem's scope, discovered that 59 percent of the pesticides either used or allowed by third world countries on ten of our most important food imports, including bananas, sugar, and tomatoes, are illegal here. The figures for coffee beans and tea are even higher—over 80 percent. Roasting coffee, however, substantially reduces pesticide residue. And the most common analytical test used by the FDA cannot even measure the amount of dangerous chemicals in much of our food.

Once overseas, especially in the third world countries that supply us with the bulk of our food imports, [these substances] enter a virtual no-man's-land as far as regulatory matters go. Third world restrictions on pesticide use are rare, and those that do exist are seldom enforced. Bribery and corruption worsen the problem.

The American consumer is not alone in being endangered. Widespread illiteracy, ignorance, and poor working conditions in developing countries also take their toll. The Natural Resources Defense Council says that roughly 750,000 people are poisoned by pesticides in these countries every year.

What is the effect on our health? The Health Effects Branch, a little-known section of the EPA, keeps a sort of running scoreboard, albeit a gruesome one, on what hazardous pesticides here and overseas are doing to us by regularly collecting human lipid (fat tissue), urine, and blood samples from points around the country. The object is to measure how many man-made chemicals are working their way into our bodies. The findings are not encouraging. Scientists are detecting an ever-escalating number of chemicals, especially as their measuring instruments become more sophisticated. DDT, aldrin, dieldrin, DBCP, heptachlor, chlordane, BHC, endrin, mirex—essentially the whole list of persistent, hazardous pesticides banned or severely restricted by the EPA—are in our bodies. Every baby born into today's world carries pesticides; the placenta is unable to screen them out. After birth, an infant continues to consume through mother's milk, which is also contaminated. (Even so, mother's milk is considered preferable to formula because of the immunities it gives to a newborn.)

EPA statistics reveal some good news, however. Since the nine-year-old ban on DDT here and despite the pesticide's continued use in much of the rest of the world, average levels in Americans' fatty tissue have fallen by about half. That fact alone makes a strong argument for government regulation.

The EPA *has* set limits for some contaminants in our food, but congressional-oversight committees and other government investigative agencies have blasted the method used as hopelessly flawed. They are right. If I eat three plums, for example, I have exceeded the amount the EPA assumes an average person eats per year when it calculates safe levels of pesticide consumption for humans. According to the EPA, the average person eats only seven and one-half ounces of plums per year. That same amount applies to other fruits and to vegetables, such as avocados, eggplant, artichokes, nectarines, raspberries, and tangerines.

Government has not paid much attention to the long-term health consequences of the residues that find their way into our diet. In the end, the consumer is left in the dark as to what pesticides are there. At the very least, food-ingredient labels should include the pesticides used in the growing. Consumers would then have a means to protect themselves.

Pesticides Bypass the Third World's Most Pressing Needs

The entire worldwide trade in hazardous pesticides... by and large bypasses the local third world need for more food for the hungry. In fact, upon close examination, pesticides are ironically contributing to the process by which hunger and malnutrition are becoming institutionalized in the third world. A recent United Nations study revealed that in 80 underdeveloped countries, only 3 percent of the landowners control about 80 percent of the land. Due to this highly-concentrated land ownership pattern, only the very rich can afford to purchase expensive petrochemical derivatives for killing agricultural pests — although the primary poisoning victims are farmworkers and their families who live on the land. Also, small farmers whose land is near the large landholdings using pesticides often have to follow suit due to the resurgence of insects which typically occurs after heavy pesticide applications. Small farmers then go into debt due to the expense of buying pesticides, a development that in turn intensifies the process by which more and more land falls into fewer and fewer hands.

The reality of pesticide use differs, therefore, from what the agrochemical industry would like us to believe. Pesticides are in fact a tool in one of the most significant historical trends of our time — the capital invasion of the third world by multinational corporations. Facing saturated markets at home, U.S. and European chemical companies, with their far-flung networks of subsidiaries and affiliates are looking to the third world for new profit opportunities.

The major consumer issues surrounding the global trade in pesticides, then, must be viewed in this overall political and economic framework. Whether or not to expand pesticide use is far more than a strictly scientific or agricultural question — it is a decision that carries significant political implications for the kind of world our children will live in.

A HEALTHY ENVIRONMENT IS A BASIC HUMAN RIGHT

In both the first and the third world, a healthy environment should be the basic right of all people, rich or poor.

Toward this goal, one of the Pesticide Action Network's top priorities is the development of alternatives to pesticide use in food production. PAN has carefully emphasized that it does not advocate an immediate halt to pesticide use. Rather, PAN believes in a phaseout of reliance on pesticides and a commitment to alternative methods of pest control, including biological controls, trap-cropping, and some of the traditional methods still employed with great success around the world like crop rotation, better tillage and soil care techniques — all labor-intensive as opposed to capital-intensive farming methods. Where organic farming methods have been seriously employed, they have proved at least as effective as chemical-intensive pest-control growing techniques. So one question for consumers is what kind of food production and distribution system is needed for non-chemical farming to proliferate?

In the third world, where many people remain on the land, one important prerequisite for cutting pesticide use is already in place — a larger proportion of growers to consumers than we currently employ in the developed world. Non-chemical farming is labor-intensive. But today, all over the world, labor is leaving the land. In the U.S. this trend is well-advanced. Two hundred years ago all but about 3 percent of the population lived on farms; today, the proportions are roughly reversed. With our huge urban centres, we have created a consumer class no longer involved in growing food. Large-scale farms, employing monocropping, mechanization and intensive chemical use, have sprung up to mass-produce food for this class. Pesticides are a key component in this system, because large areas planted in single crops are much more vulnerable to attacks from various pests than were the former small-plot, varied crop farms of our past.

Many third world countries still have time to avoid some of the worst excesses of our model of social organization. Small units of control over farms producing for smaller regional urban units clearly is a more rational way to organize society, given the political, economic, and environmental implications of the alternative.

Pesticides, furthermore, carry many other risks that must be considered when deciding to employ them as tools for growing more food.

The resurgence of malaria in Central America, on the Indian subcontinent and elsewhere has been tied to the resistance to DDT of malaria-carrying mosquitoes in those areas.

Despite 40 years of escalating use of pesticides, not one pest species has been wiped out anywhere in the world. Instead, both pests and predator populations are devastated initially, with only a few strong individuals surviving. These few however, are now resistant to the pesticide, and lacking their natural predators, they quickly proliferate. Soon, we are back where we started, or worse, as far as the number of pests are concerned, and we have incurred a large expense and the contamination of people and the environment in the process.

CONSUMERS HAVE THE RIGHT TO PROTECTION, TOO

There are, therefore, many different kinds of problems connected with the current explosion of pesticide use in our time. Sometimes living as we do in the midst of this chemical blizzard we cannot see the route that we must follow to get out. But it is imperative that consumer activists, environmentalists, farmers and workers work together to find that path out of our current mess. Because as bad as the situation may now be, we are literally only on the threshold of the chemical age. The volume of chemicals released into the American environment alone over the coming decade, for example, is expected to double.

Finally, summarizing the pesticide issue from a consumer forcus, we can see how the present chaos in the global pesticides trade violates consumer rights in two fundamental ways. Consumers' right to safety is being violated every day. Ten years ago, according to World Health Organization estimates, somebody somewhere in the world was being poisoned on the average of every minute. Today, due to increased pesticide use everywhere, someone is poisoned on the average of every 42 seconds.

Secondly, the right to be informed — to be protected against fraudulent or misleading advertising, labeling and sales practices — is being widely violated by the multinational agrochemical companies, particularly in the third world.

There has been widescale failure by governmental authorities to curb pesticide proliferation. Therefore we as concerned citizens of the global environment must act before it is too late.

— *David Weir*

Back on the Family Farm, a Non-chemical Alternative

by Linda Siskind

Most farmers depend on pesticides. For one thing, they may be the only way a farmer has ever heard of to protect crops. For another, they do knock out those pests.

The key is economics. Pesticides in legalese are even called "economic poisons." What with the increasing debts incurred by farmers for equipment and fuel and the rising cost of farm land, it's more important than ever that crops prosper. A Nebraska farmer speaks for many when he says pesticides provide "the cheapest insurance I can get." Chemicals are regarded as *the* way to take one risk out of what is still a very risky business.

Nine out of ten farmers in California say they get their advice about pest control directly from chemical company employees. These employees are licensed by the state as "pest control advisers" who go out to the field, pronounce a pest problem, and recommend a chemical solution. A farmer doesn't even have to (and sometimes doesn't) go out to the field to see the problem. The advisor does it all for him.

Chemical agricultural companies have the market all sown up, you might say, but there's still plenty of promotion going on. Maybe this is because there are too many poisons around that do the same thing. Like detergents, they must be pushed with heavy advertising. Sometimes the companies put on a show for the whole town at once. They give away free hats, raffle off a vest, present a slide show.

There's more to pesticide use than that, though. Banks may loan money for equipment only if they see "traditional" (thirty-year-old) farming practices being used (i.e., chemical farming). Likewise, insurance companies may insure against crop loss only if the farmer follows the "traditional" advice of the pesticide salesman. Packers and processors who buy the produce when it is grown may require that no blemishes appear, and set "cosmetic standards" achievable only with heavy chemical use. Even the farmers themselves may set standards to be perfect, knowing this is hard to attain, in order to keep supply low and prices high.

Heavy pesticide use is also assured by pesticide application contracts which call for a certain regimen of spraying, etc., based on the calendar rather than the presence of a pest in the field, and by spraying pesticides by airplane. Wind may send up to sixty percent of the pesticide miles away from target, wasting not only the pesticide but also the farmers' money, and covering their fields with chemicals that can do them harm.

Whatever the reasons, the results are the same: an overuse of pesticides. Reports from the government and environmental groups agree that farmers could earn the same money using perhaps as little as one-half of the pesticides they use now.

They say this is because there are alternatives to blanket pesticide use which cost less, use less energy and present fewer hazards to the environment and to human health. Perhaps even more important, they worry about pesticide use because farmers are losing twice as much of their crops now than they did thirty years ago—after using twelve times more pesticides.

What is happening in the fields? Pesticides are too strong for the job. They kill everything—including the original pests, the pests' enemies or predators, and other bugs quietly munching along unnoticed. The spray may seem to take care of most of the original pests, but if the predators' food or shelter is gone too, the way is clear for the original pests which survive to multiply and take over with a vengeance. This is known as pest resurgence.

The farmers' next step is to spray some more. Ultimately, the pests develop resistance to the poison used so a new poison must be found. And the cycle repeats itself with a different pesticide, different species—resurgence, secondary outbreak, resistance.

INTEGRATED PEST MANAGEMENT

As for pesticide alternatives, most common is a group of farming practices known as Integrated Pest Management, or IPM. Key to IPM is actually counting what pests are in the field, seeing what natural enemies are there, and figuring out what it would cost to control the pest compared to letting it do some minimum of damage. When the decision is made to go ahead and attack pests, the method of choice is biological control (letting predators destroy each other, sterilizing insects, etc.), developing pest-resistant strains, and practicing preventive medicine by cleaning stagnant breeding water, diversifying crops to contain pest outbreaks, and planning an early harvest. Pesticides may be used when none of these methods is enough.

The trouble is that not enough people are trained to implement IPM on a large scale, and IPM methods on some crops are too experimental to convince farmers to switch when there's lots of cash at stake. Also, IPM promotes such a different concept (let some bugs live) from the usual knockout approach of pesticides, that it has its bitter enemies. The chairman of California's

---

Reprinted with permission from The Pesticide Syndrome, *Earthwork Publications, Center for Rural Studies, Minneapolis, MN 1979.*

Assembly Agricultural Committee, for example, told a reporter, "If some textbook expert comes and tells me to wait for the good bugs while my crop is eaten by bad bugs, I think I would spray him instead."

Beyond IPM, some farmers say trying to kill pests is not the answer to pest control problems. They say that pest control consists of seeking only short-term solutions to essentially long-term problems of soil depletion. From intensive use of chemicals and continuous cultivation, the soils lose something, they say. And from these soils, only weak plants will grow, plants that are more susceptible to injury from both disease and insect infestation.

Says twenty five-year veteran farmer Jack Grimmer, "We have these plants that might look green because they've got a lot of nitrogen in them, but the plants aren't all that healthy. . . .The major culprit is the fact that farmers have neglected their soils. . . . Our soils have been depleted. We've basically mined them, exploited them just like the multinationals do in other countries. We've done that with our own soil."

What sold Grimmer on trying a different style of farming after twenty-five years was seeing some "eco-ag" corn grown in Colorado. (Eco-ag is a form of organic farming.) The nodes on the eco-ag corn plants were clean; nodes on a neighboring chemically-treated plant were all clogged up. The purity of the eco-ag plant and the fact that the farmer was getting a premium price for it convinced Jack to give it a try himself.

The Grimmers and their neighbors are also worried about the health aspects of using chemicals. "If we don't stop the chemical feast we aren't going to be around to even enjoy whatever we have."

ORGANIC—AND PROFITABLE

Money is one big reason Russel Wolter farms organically in the Monterey area. Wolter was recently featured in *New West* magazine because his produce was the only produce tested by the magazine from health food stores and Safeway that actually contained no detectable traces of insecticides. Wolter says that when he started farming, he just didn't have the money for pesticides. Now, his costs without chemicals are similar to the costs of conventional farming, sometimes less.

"I envision," says Jack Grimmer, "that in ten years, if we have anything to say about it, in northern California there won't be any more chemicals. None. It will happen for no other reason than a neighbor looking across the road—like discovering gold, you can't keep it quiet. Old Joe at the crossroads says, 'Gees, I haven't seen you spray but once all summer. What the hell.' I say, 'That's eco-farming people.' I tell him that now, he laughs (hahaha) but pretty soon he looks over there and says, 'Boy, those beets sure look good.' or, 'That corn looks good. What'd that corn make?' 'Aw, made about 100 sacks.' 'What?!'

"That's going to do the job. He may think that the chemicals in the food is all hokem and he might not even care. But there's one thing that that farmer does care about and that's his pocketbook. So if he sees you making more money than he is on a crop per acre, that's going to bug him to death..."

Meanwhile, most farmers are convinced by the information at their disposal that the only way they can keep ahead is by using chemicals, and so they spray.

THE LAND MOURNS

Therefore the land mourns,
  and all who dwell in it languish,
And also the beasts of the field,
  and the birds of the air;
  And even the fish of the sea are taken away.
                    (Hosea 4:3)

CREATION SUFFERS

...and nature's majesty is slowly being destroyed, but the choices and changes are still ours to make. The following report explains where the plague of acid rain begins, and what it is doing to life on earth.

It sounds like a screenplay for a science fiction movie: a planet where invisible gases undergo a transformation as they travel among the clouds, eventually falling to earth — sometimes thousands of kilometres from their source — as acids capable of crippling and killing the environments they invade. But this, unfortunately, is the chilling reality of what is happening at this very moment throughout North America and Scandinavia especially, as well as in other countries.

Watching the rain drop gently onto a remote lake a thousand kilometres from the nearest industrial center, it is difficult to look at the rainbow forming in the misty sunlight and accept that what has just fallen is slowly killing most of the life within that innocent body of water. But already, in Canada and the United States, thousands of rivers and lakes are "dead" — no longer able to support fish and plant populations — and many thousands more are endangered. In Norway and Sweden, where the damage is more advanced, the total is in tens of thousands.

The problem is acid rain, an insidious but deadly pollution resulting from industrial combustion. As well as killing fish populations and aquatic vegetation, it threatens forests, crops and soils; erodes building and automobile surfaces; and may be a danger to human health.

The forecast for the immediate and distant future is bleak. The present and potential destruction caused by acid rain is staggering, both economically and aesthetically. The consequences of not ending this man-made pollution are simply not acceptable.

But we are not helpless or without hope, for the problem can be solved. What human beings have started, human beings can stop. That decision, however, will have to be made by us.

WHERE DOES ACID RAIN COME FROM?

It begins in the towering smokestacks of smelters and fossil-fueled power plants, oil refineries and other industrial funnels; and in the exhaust pipes of millions of overused cars that clog our major cities. Daily, thousands of tons of invisible gas — the oxides of sulfur and nitrogen primarily — stream into the atmosphere, following the winds on a journey that can last as long as several weeks (although on average they remain aloft for two to five days) and take them thousands of kilometres from their point of origin.

As these invisible clouds of sulfur dioxide and nitrogen oxides journey in the wind currents, enough time passes for chemical reactions to take place which convert them into acid-causing sulfates and nitrates. While the conversion of sulfur dioxide is rather slow, nitrogen oxides may be transformed more quickly.

As every grade school child knows from watching teacher toss an apple into the air in imitation of Sir Isaac Newton, what goes up — inevitable — must come back down. For sulfuric acid and nitric acid, the return trip to the earth's surface comes with every rainstorm and snowfall of the seasons. Mixing with the water vapor in the clouds, they eventually tumble down to earth as acid rain and acid snow.

Sulfur dioxide (SO_2) contributes about 70 percent of the problem while nitrogen oxides (NO_x) account for most of the rest. In Canada, sulfur dioxide comes primarily from smelters such as those of the International Nickel Company (INCO) plant in Sudbury, Ontario; or from the various Ontario Hydro fossil-fueled power plants throughout that province. In the United States, most SO_2 originates from the burning of fossil fuels such as oils and coal to produce electricity. The largest such emission area is the upper Ohio valley (eastern Ohio, northern West Virginia, and western Pennsylvania) where high-sulfur coal is burned with little control over the amount of sulfur dioxide emitted.

In both countries, about half of the NO_x emissions come from the transportation sector, particularly from the tailpipes of moving vehicles. Electrical utilities and other combustion sources account for the rest.

LONG RANGE TRANSPORTATION

Most acid materials fall to earth within a few hundred to a few thousand kilometres from their point of origin.

From Downwind: The Acid Rain Story, *published by Environment Canada, 1982. Reprinted with permission.*

This provides time for them to cross state, provincial and international borders, creating an environmental and political problem that is not dealt with in existing legislation among the world's countries.

The United States is the largest producer of sulfur dioxide in the world, emitting 25.7 million tons a year, compared to Canada's total of 5 million tons. Because of the prevailing winds, large quantities of American SO_2 are blown into Canada, falling on areas such as Muskoka-Haliburton, the heartland of Ontario's tourist industry; onto Quebec, which is extremely acid-sensitive; and as far east as Nova Scotia and Newfoundland.

Says Dr. Douglas Whelpdale of Environment Canada's Atmospheric Environment Service, the scientific body responsible for tracking acid rain in Canada, "The studies we have done lead us to believe that about half of the sulfur coming into the atmosphere over eastern Canada comes from the United States." But it is not just a one-way street. "We send back an amount equal to about one-quarter to maybe a third of what they send us."

DROWNING WORMS

Dr. Harold Harvey, a professor of zoology at the University of Toronto, stood on a hill overlooking Lumsden Lake in Ontario and sighed as he watched the picture postcard scene below him. In the middle of a lake a lone fisherman slouched peacefully in a boat, enjoying the pleasure of his solitude as the sun winked off the tips of the sheer blue water. "As I looked down," recalls Harvey, "all I could think of was, the poor guy doesn't know it, but he's not fishing. All he's doing is drowning worms."

It is a chilling and ironic twist that as a lake acidifies it becomes more attractive; for as the various life forms within it die off, the water clears and appears to be in radiant health — until you look beneath the surface. This sinister paradox has also made it difficult to rouse attention to the problem. "If you look at a stream or lake and you see an old tire in it or it stinks, then it's easier to demonstrate to people that in fact there is some environmental damage being done," says Ron Reid of the Federation of Ontario Naturalists. "But if it's crystal clear and it looks beautiful, it's so difficult to see the effects."

It is not the result of a single storm that makes acid rain so harmful. The acids are too diluted for that to happen. Rather, it is the slow and insidious buildup over a long period of time, the "loading" effect, that gradually wears away the ability of an environment to neutralize the constant doses of acid.

Some parts of the United States and Canada have a natural capacity to neutralize the acid, usually a limestone base in the soil or water body. But large sections of northeastern United States and eastern Canada, especially, do not — and they are extremely vulnerable.

ATMOSPHERIC DUMPING GROUND

"The Adirondacks are an atmospheric dumping ground," says Anne LaBastille, a commissioner with the Adirondacks Parks Agency in New York. "The acid rain comes from the Ohio River valley basin and we're the first high land it hits."

In the early 1970s, Carl Schofield of Cornell University went into the Adirondacks to study the lakes that nestle peacefully among the rugged mountains. The results of his tests were shocking: 51 percent of the lakes at an elevation of more than 600 metres had a pH below 5. Comparable data from the period 1920-37 showed that only 4 percent of the lakes were below pH 5 at that time.

Entire communities of brook trout, lake trout, white sucker, brown bullhead and other species were wiped out, gone in a period of approximately 40 years. Recent tests by Schofield indicate the problem is worsening. "I estimated that about 200 lakes were dead when I did my tests initially." he says. "But that figure is much higher now. And it's no longer just lakes at a high elevation. It's now at all levels."

The acidity attacks the fish populations in several ways. As the pH of the lake decreases, it alters the delicately balanced working of the internal system of the fish. One result is a depletion of calcium from the bone tissue and skeleton. "Because of that, a lot of the fish you find in these lakes are deformed, humpbacked, or dwarfed," says Dr. Thomas Hutchinson of the University of Toronto.

Another unnatural killer stalking the waters is aluminum. The acidity causes it to be released from surrounding soils and it is then easily taken into the gills of the fish. "The aluminum gradually clogs up the gills." says Hutchinson. "Basically, they die very slowly and eventually sink to the bottom. It can take years." Studies have actually recorded fish sneezing in an attempt to clear their gills.

The last blow to the lake comes long after the fish and plant populations are gone. Eventually, the only life the lake can support are thick mats of algae, moss and fungus which cover the bottom of the lake. "The Swedish experience is that the lakes look like they've got Astroturf on the bottom when they're finished," says Dr. Harvel.

STATUES AND ARCHITECTURE

For 2500 years the Caryatids, six marble maidens carved by the sculptor Phidias in the 5th century B.C., supported the famous Erechtheum Porch of the Acropolis, in Athens, on their delicate shoulders. Unflinching in the face of centuries of weather, wars, and old age, they graced the ruins of the ancient Greek capital with their noble sense of duty.

In 1977, however, the six maidens were removed to a museum and replaced with fiberglass replicas because their ancient marble was turning into soft gypsum. The reason? Air pollution, and particularly acid-causing pollutants. Acid rain.

In cities throughout the world, some of the oldest and most glorious architectural structures are being mutilated beyond recognition by acid rain. The ancient Egyptian granite obelisk, Cleopatra's Needle (circa 1500 B.C.), suffered serious surface flaking from two years of exposure to air pollution in New York City after surviving relatively unscathed for all those centuries in Egypt. The Parthenon, the Taj Mahal and the Colosseum in Rome are all suffering from this unnatural erosion. Landmarks such as the Lincoln Memorial and Washington Monument in Washington, gravestones, rock art, building surfaces and automobiles are all feeling the bite of constant acid washings. The President's Council on Environmental Quality estimated in 1979 that the annual cost to the United States in architectural damage was upwards of $2 billion.

DANGER TO HUMAN HEALTH

As yet, there is little direct evidence of how acid rain affects human health, but there are enough clues and early warning signals to suggest that in the long run, the danger to human health may be a most serious consequence of not stopping acid rain.

As the winds carrying acidic substances speed across the countryside, other pollutants often hitch a ride: heavy metals such as mercury, lead, zinc and copper. These metals come from industrial emissions and automobiles and when they are deposited on lakes can be toxic to fish.

Increased acidity also releases heavy metal from soils, and scientists appearing before an Ontario committee reported there are increased levels of heavy metals in lakes which are acidifying. "In cases where neither the acidity nor the metals are toxic by themselves," the committee's report also notes, "the combination can be deadly. Fish that are able to survive in waters with heavy metal concentrations are often unfit for human consumption." These heavy metals could also be a threat to human health if they exist in areas where drinking water is obtained from an untreated supply.

WHAT CAN BE DONE ABOUT ACID RAIN?

How can this be stopped? "The solution is very straightforward," says John Roberts, Minister of the Environment in Canada. "We must reduce drastically the amount of acid-causing pollution that is being emitted in both countries. I am told it is technically possible to effect such reductions. The only stumbling block is cost. How much and by whom?"

The technology does indeed exist. Emission controls can be placed on smokestacks and cars; and coal, which is a main culprit responsible for SO_2 emissions, can be washed in order to cut down on the sulfur sent into the atmosphere.

The argument against implementing these readily available solutions is that it will cost too much. The price tag is considerable; and in these days of high energy costs and belt-tightening budgets, both industry and government are cautious when it comes to spending money — especially on preventive medicine. But the cost of not taking action far surpasses the price of emission controls. Industries such as forestry, tourism, and fishing are threatened; building and automobile surfaces are deteriorating every day; health costs could be astronomical in the long run. At every turn there are jobs which could be lost and resources which may never be replenished. When the less tangible effects are added — the aesthetic losses, for example — the argument against not taking immediate action seems economically unsound and foolish.

WHAT CAN I DO?

"No one has the right at any time to endanger the environmental health of a nation or continent," says John Roberts. To that end, the Canadian and American governments have signed an agreement to begin the complex task of trying to stop the flow of acid rain across the international border.

Meantime, citizens need not sit back passively and wait. If people make it known to government and industry that there can be no trade-offs for the environment, that they, as consumers, are not willing to let lower prices or convenience take dominion over the land, that message will be heard. They can convey that message directly to their elected representatives or they can actively support one of the many environmental groups. But if no cry is heard in the legislatures or in the corporate boardrooms, the people making the decisions that will affect the quality of life in North America for a long, long time may presume that they can act as they alone see fit.

CLEANING UP THE CAUSES

by Larry Tye

Over the last few years, several European governments have taken the lead in enforcing strict controls over polluters and restricting practices that endanger the environment and life itself. Larry Tye, a reporter for the Louisville Courier-Journal, recently toured facilities in West Germany and Norway to find out why and how the acid rain that is killing Europe's forests and lakes is being attacked more vigorously than that endangering North America's natural heritage.

Senior environmental officials from 36 nations met in Geneva, Switzerland, in 1979 to discuss acid rain—the broadest dialogue ever held on the issue.

President Jimmy Carter's U.S. delegation, eager to clean up emissions, found itself mediating conflicts that divided the Europeans. West Germany, one of Europe's worst air polluters, believed that too little was known about acid rain to decide how to control it. Norway, whose lakes had been devastated by acid rain, insisted on an immediate, aggressive cleanup program.

The 36 nations followed a middle line laid down by the United States: They agreed to consider ways to cut acid emissions, but delayed any action.

Since then, the U.S. government has lost interest in stopping acid rain and done nothing to implement the modest Geneva agreement, saying too little is known about the problem to begin solving it.

West Germany, meanwhile, has made a dramatically different turnaround: Today it is one of Norway's strongest allies in pushing for emission controls, much to the satisfaction of its neighbor to the north.

So as the United States idly watches, Norway demonstrates how acid rain is caused, how it travels and how it wreaks havoc upon lakes and forests, while West Germany shows how the pollution can be cleaned up.

The evidence that led to Germany's stunning reversal on acid rain is in the yellow needles that cover the snow in the Black Forest. *Schwarzwald,* as it is known, is immense, covering 2,500 square miles in southwestern West Germany. It is also mountainous.

But the Black Forest's most distinguishing characteristic — to the millions who have read about it in German literature and thousands who have visited it each year — has been the unusual hue that gave it its name. The forest was so crowded with firs, spruce and other trees that sunlight was blocked. It was black as pitch.

Today, however, the needle cover on the snow is too thick and too yellow. The trees are too brown, the treetops far too thin. But what stands out most is how far you can see through distant lines of trees — and how much sun shines back at you. The forest is no longer black.

In 1982, the Germans conducted their first federal forest study and found that 8 percent of Germany's trees — covering 1.4 million acres — were hurt. The damage was widespread, which tended to rule out localized causes like fungi or fights among species. More and more German scientists acknowledged that air pollution contributed to the problem.

Four weeks after the damage survey was released, the West German government announced a program to cut sulfur dioxide pollution by 60 percent over the next decade. Nitrogen oxides, the other major source of acid rain, would be reduced by about 40 percent. It was the world's most aggressive program to eliminate acid rain, stronger even than the most ambitious effort being considered by the U.S. Congress.

"Environmental protection costs money," says Dr. Richard Lammel, a senior official responsible for implementing Kohl's acid-rain control program. "But in the long run it pays. If you destroy what you live on you can't have economic progress."

The program has been helped by Germans' love for their woodlands. "To the normal German the forest is mainly something in the mind — it's not practical, not economic," said Riederer von Paar, president of the German Foresters Association. "Forests seem to be the last area where people can feel free."

Another important supporter of the cleanup is the forestry industry. Dying forests mean about $250 million a year in lost income from timber, paper and other products, Lammel said.

Today Germany has strict new standards for all plants — large and small, old and new. Large plants have to cut 85 percent of sulfur from their emissions, midsized plants 60 percent and small plants have to use low-sulfur

---

Copyright © 1984. The Courier-Journal. *Reprinted with permission.*

fuel. West Germany is now as tough as the United States on new plants, and it is tougher on older plants. Those in Germany are required to have scrubbers; older U.S. plants aren't. The difference is key: U.S. government studies show that, unless controls are put on old plants, acid-rain problems will persist into the next century.

The Germans also are requiring cars sold after 1986 to have catalytic converters and to use unleaded gasoline, which will eliminate about 30 percent of Germany's nitrogen oxide pollution. Also impressive is the German acid-rain research program.

Yet even with all these programs, Germany is limited in how much it can do to solve its acid-rain problem. That's because half of its air pollution is produced by France, Britain, Switzerland and other countries. West Germany has thus set out to persuade them, particularly Britain, to follow its lead.

Germany is asking the other nine members of the European Community to install scrubbers on their plants and to use unleaded gasoline in their cars. It is also trying to persuade the United States and other non-European nations to do the same.

"It's our duty to show you people what's going on here," said Riederer von Paar, president of the German Foresters Association. "You should start on controls before it gets as bad as here. We lost so much time."

LEARNING FROM NORWAY

Unlike Germany, Norway can't do much to eliminate its air pollution because nearly all of it blows in from elsewhere. In many ways, Norway is a victim in Europe as are Canada and the northeast United States in North America.

And Norway has highly advanced research to prove

its case. Norwegian studies show that sulfur and nitrogen pollutants fall as acid rain long distances from where they are produced and that cutting emission of these pollutants will rejuvenate dying and dead lakes.

The first point was easy to prove: There's little industry — and few people — in southern Norway.

The Norwegians can also predict, based on exhaustive tests, how much reduction in acidity will revive a lake. Merete Johannessen, a scientist at the Norwegian Institute for Water Research, explains the importance of that:

"When you address yourselves to foreign countries producing acid rain and say 'Stop it,' they ask, 'Will it help?' We can now provide answers. A 30 percent reduction in acid rain over 10 years would bring back to life 20 percent of the acidified lakes (in Norway)."

Norwegians also have studied whether adding lime to dying lakes is worth the expense and effort. This approach, which is used in Sweden and some parts of the United States, is a key element of the U.S. government's plan.

The Norwegian conclusion: "You can do it in specific...areas where people are motivated to do it themselves," Johannessen said. "But liming is like aspirin. It brings the lake from one polluted state to another. The only solution is to reduce emissions."

The U.S. and Canadian governments have acknowledged the importance of Norways' research by helping pay for it. In return, Norwegians have focused attention on American and Canadian problems, and they've found parallels with Norway.

Lou Curth of Riparius, N.Y. learned how acid rain could soil a pristine environment during a visit to Scandinavia 10 years ago. "I remember going out with my wife's brother ice fishing. You could see the scum on the ice. The soot settled right on the ice."

But Curth, a New York forest ranger, never thought he'd see a similar trail of pollution in his own back yard in the middle of the 6 million-acre Adirondack Park.

The realization that he was wrong came slowly and began with the lakes.

"That's the problem with acid rain. It sneaks up on you. You start to go fishing and don't get anything, but you don't know why it's happening. The whole food chain is disrupted. For a short time you get trophy-size trout because their competition for food is gone. You think this is great, but then all of a sudden everything disappears. Once they're gone it's all over.

"The next question on everyone's mind is that a lot of people live here because they think it's a clean healthy place to live. If acid rain is doing this to aquatic life and the forests, what about people? Nobody has answered that question yet, I'm afraid."

In June, 1983 a panel of scientists — appointed by President Reagan to review U.S.-Canadian acid-rain research — concluded, "If we take the conservative point of view that we must wait until the scientific knowledge is definitive, the accumulated deposition and damaged environment may reach the point of irreversibility."

A year after the 1979 conference in Geneva, Carter signed a pact with Canada committing the two countries to negotiate a cutback on sulfur emissions. Douglas Costle, Carter's EPA head, told governors they might have to cut air pollution to reduce Canada's acid rain. Carter and Costle asserted that acid rain caused major damage; that sulfur dioxide and nitrogen oxides can be carried over long distances, and that America must share responsibility for cleaning them up.

But the progress ceased soon after President Reagan took office. Negotiations slowed, and key scientists were replaced on study groups set up after the 1980 accord. Canada offered to cut in half its sulfur emissions if the United States would do the same — but Reagan officials rejected the offer in June 1982, saying too little is known about acid rain's causes. But researchers across the United States, while agreeing there is much they don't know, insist they can document many of air pollution's insidious inroads into the well-being of lakes, trees and people. They say this warrants at least some immediate steps to eliminate the pollution.

Says Lou Curth, the New York forest ranger: "It's ridiculous. There's so much evidence of the damage and so many people being hurt we just can't afford to let it go on this way. The time has passed for this studying business."

POISONS IN THE EARTH

Unless we take steps to reduce the production of hazardous waste, environmental problems will multiply in the future.

by Deborah A. Sheiman

Consider the facts. There are an estimated 15,000 abandoned hazardous waste dumps spread across the country, the legacy of past mismanagement. Some 50 percent of the hazardous waste generated today escapes control under the present regulatory framework. And every year another 264 million metric tons more hazardous waste is added to the environment's stockpile for the future. Hazardous waste management involves political questions, and informed citizens should have a voice in the outcome.

WHAT ARE HAZARDOUS WASTES?

Hazardous wastes are industrial byproducts that pose a substantial threat or potential hazard to human health or the environment when improperly handled. Industries produce some 264 million metric tons of hazardous waste each year, or approximately 71 billion gallons. The U.S. Environmental Protection Agency (EPA) has identified certain manufacturing processes that produce hazardous waste and specific toxic constituents that render waste hazardous. Waste may also be designated hazardous if it has any of four characteristics—toxicity, reactivity, ignitability or corrosivity.

Toxic wastes can cause acute health effects—poisoning, chemical burns, and nervous system disorders or chronic, long-term problems such as cancer, birth defects or sterility. Examples of toxic wastes include heavy metals such as cadmium and lead and synthetic organic compounds such as pesticides and PCBs.

Reactive wastes tend to explode easily or give off toxic fumes. Reactions maybe caused by exposure to air, water, heat or shock. Obsolete munitions and manufacturing wastes from the explosives and chemical industries are examples of reactive wastes.

Ignitable wastes present a fire hazard because they tend to undergo spontaneous combustion at relatively low temperatures. Examples include discarded organic solvents such as toluene and benzene, oils, plasticizers, some pesticides and paint and varnish removers.

About 10-15 percent of all industrial waste produced is hazardous. Industries that produce the bulk of hazardous by-products (in descending order of volume of wastes generated) are: the organic chemicals, textiles, petroleum refining and rubber and plastic industries.

Another major source of hazardous waste is the Department of Defense, which has stockpiled thousands of tons of obsolete explosives, herbicides and nerve gas. Disposal of banned substances such as PCBs and certain pesticides also presents difficult problems. Households and retailers must dispose of smaller quantities of expired medicines and paints, and farmers need to discard used pesticide containers. Hospitals, research labs and service stations are still other sources of hazardous waste.

From a geographic perspective, the more industrialized states of the mid-Atlantic and Great Lakes region, along with California, Texas and Tennessee, generate the largest volume of industrial hazardous wastes. These states house the largest number of priority dumpsites eligible for cleanup under the federal Superfund law; New Jersey, New York and Pennsylvania top the list. To date, EPA has designated 546 sites for its national priority list of those dumpsites deserving prompt cleanup. However, the Congressional Office of Technology Assessment estimates that as many as 15,000 sites spread across the country will push clean-up costs into the billions of dollars.

Meanwhile, only about 10 percent of the hazardous waste currently being generated is disposed of in an environmentally sound manner. The rest threatens our water quality, our air quality, and our marine and land-based life support systems.

HOW DO HAZARDOUS WASTES CAUSE DAMAGE?

Each phase of the life cycle of a hazardous waste, from "cradle to grave," presents the opportunity for exposure

---

Deborah Sheiman is Senior Specialist for Natural Resources, the League of Women Voters, 1720 M Street, N.W., Washington, D.C. 20036; Reprinted by permission from Engage/Social Action, Vol. 12, No. 10, October 1984.

to humans and the environment. Fires, explosions and accidental releases may occur during the storage, transportation, treatment and disposal of wastes. The transportation phase is particularly accident-prone. Highway and rail accidents occur most frequently, sometimes forcing massive evacuations of nearby populations. Spills from ships and barges, though less costly in human lives, present a severe hazard to natural ecosystems.

Groundwater contamination, through leaching from landfills and surface impoundments, is the most common type of environmental pollution due to waste mismanagement. Contaminated aquifers threaten drinking water and irrigation supplies. Once contamination occurs, it becomes difficult, oftentimes impossible, to restore an aquifer to its original condition.

Surface water pollution becomes another source of exposure to hazardous waste. Runoff from storage and disposal areas and overflow of toxic waste treatment lagoons can pollute lakes and streams.

Air pollution causes exposure whenever open burning, evaporation or wind erosion of wastes occurs at a land disposal site. Poorly controlled incineration at land or at sea provides an additional source of airborne exposure.

The health effects of exposure to toxic substances fall into two general categories—acute and chronic. Acute effects can occur from a single exposure. Persons can die from inhalation of toxic fumes and absorption of toxins through the skin. Chemical skin burns and blindness are other severe and often irreversible health effects. More common are reversible effects, such as skin and eye irritation and the acute symptoms of poisoning—headaches, nausea, dizziness, blurred vision and tremors.

Chronic effects are associated with repeated exposures—in the workplace, at home, through ingestion of contaminated food and water, or breathing polluted air. Chronic effects include cancer, birth defects, sterility, decreased immune function and heart, lung and liver damage. Some of these effects may not show up for many years after exposure.

Improper waste management practices can also threaten the environment. Accounts of fish kills and livestock losses are only symptoms of the larger problem. The impacts of contamination on essential ecological process and interrelationships, such as nutrient cycling, soil formation and the provision of critical habitats, become harder to qualify. As with human toxicology, living organisms are threatened not only by direct mortality but by chronic affects such as alteration of genetic material, behavioral disorders, and reproductive failure, all of which can also effect long-term survival rates.

WHAT CAN WE DO WITH IT?

Given the potential for adverse effects from hazardous wastes, we need to limit exposures. We can attack the problem at its source and restrict production or use of a toxic substance; such action has occurred in a few cases. But many other hazardous materials are still being manufactured, and still others are being generated as the leftovers of industrial processes. Private and public sector officials who want to deal with hazardous waste problems in a responsible way need to undertake a hierarchical approach to waste management that explores these questions in a systematic fashion:

• How can industrial processes be changed to reduce or eliminate production of hazardous by-products?

• Are less hazardous substitutes available?

• Can hazardous materials be recovered from the waste and recycled?

• What chemical, biological, physical or thermal treatment processes are available to destroy the waste or reduce its hazard?

• Will treatment result in a residual sludge, ash or concentrated waste that has to be disposed of?

• Which long-term storage or disposal alternative is appropriate and where is the best site?

In a free-enterprise economy, manufacturers and waste handlers who choose a sounder but more expensive waste management strategy face a competitive disadvantage. As a result, cost, rather than environmental considerations, often dictates waste management choices. Unfortunately, the existing federal regulatory framework, under the Resource Conservation and Recovery Act (RCRA) and other environmental laws,is sorely inadequate. Thus, government regulations have been largely unsuccessful to date in providing incentives for environmentally sound waste management practices.

The bulk of the hazardous waste generated today is still disposed of in or on the land. According to a recent EPA survey, underground injection is the dominant disposal method for hazardous waste and landfills are the second most commonly used method.

Both houses of the 98th Congress approved amendments to RCRA, the major federal law governing waste management. The amendments would take a first step toward shifting the balance of prevalent waste management practices from land disposal to reduction of wastes at the source. These amendments establish waste reduction as the national policy and offer a number of concrete steps to move away from reliance on unsafe, outmoded land disposal methods.

For instance, the amendments would place restrictions on the types of wastes that could be located and on construction and monitoring requirements. The more stringent requirements would have the effect of increasing the costs of land disposal, thus creating an incentive for industries to explore waste reduction alternatives.

Is There a Dump in *Your* Backyard?

Many people find out about local hazardous dumps by accident: either they observe something suspicious and investigate further, or they discover this knowledge by reading or hearing about it. That's how Love Canal got started. A small item appeared in the paper describing how the Love Canal site had been used as a chemical dump years before by Hooker Chemical and other companies. Residents put together the existence of the town and sick children and investigated further.

You can watch for physical signs: odd colored or smelling water, dead or "stressed" vegetation, dying or sick animals, odors in the air, barrels sticking out of the ground. It pays to watch for such signs and to ask a lot of questions when you spot them. When you have such suspicions, you can then take two further "action steps."

• Determine who owns, and owned in the past, the property where you spot these signs. Records of ownership are public information in your town or county. Check with your local, county or state environmental and health agencies to see if they have records or issued any licenses for chemical dumping.

• Begin to ask for environmental tests of the soil and water. Citizens Clearinghouse for Hazardous Waste (CCHW) can help you to figure out what types of tests make sense and how to make sure they are properly carried out.

If you feel that improper or illegal dumping is occurring, another "action step" that works is to set up a "Community Toxic Watch," where neighbors agree to watch for trucks, dumping and other suspicious behavior and meet regularly to compare results.

If you do have a problem, you now really need to put "action" into your "action steps." Do some research. Set up a research committee aimed at answering two questions:

• Who's responsible for causing this problem? Who was the dumper? Who let them do it?

• Who's got the power to solve the problem? Who's got the power to give you what you want?

Your group now has come to the point of decision on what it wants done about the problem. Follow this two-step process: (1) In very positive terms, ask what your group stands for (what are its guiding principles?); (2) ask what specific action your group wants the responsible parties to take.

As you work on the first step, consider CCHW's guiding principles:

• *RIGHT TO BE SAFE FROM HARMFUL EXPOSURE.* People have the inherent right to be safe in their homes and workplaces. Our children have the right to grow up strong and healthy, not diseased or deformed or to die before they've had a chance to live. They have a right to be safe in their schools, free from cancer-causing asbestos or other hazards, and to play in their backyards free from erupting chemical pits or contaminated soils.

• *RIGHT TO KNOW.* We have the right to know what poisons other people, industry, corporate polluters and government have decided to bring into our neighborhoods and workplaces. We also have the right to know how these chemicals can adversely affect our health, our environment.

• *RIGHT TO CLEANUP.* We have the right to safe, total cleanup of hazardous waste sites and spills, to have the cleanups take place quickly with our neighbors, homes and environment restored to the way they were before the polluters chose to contaminate them with chemical poisons.

• *RIGHT TO PARTICIPATE.* We have the right to participate, *as equals,* in decisions affecting our lives, children, homes and jobs on the matter of exposure to hazardous wastes. We have the right to access, without cost, to information and assistance that will make our participation meaningful and to have our needs and concerns be the major factor in *all* policy decisions.

• *RIGHT TO COMPENSATION.* We have the right to be compensated for damages to our health, our homes and our livelihoods.

• *RIGHT TO PREVENTION.* We have the right to public policy that *prevents* toxic pollution from entering our neighborhoods by using existing technology beginning with reduction at the source—a technology that will provide jobs, business opportunities and conservation of valuable resources.

DEVELOPING YOUR ACTION PLAN

Next, your group should develop its action plan, its strategy for achieving its goals. Since you now know what the problem is, who's responsible for causing it, what you want done about it and who's got the power to do it, you must now decide how you will get what you want.

Many local groups can get sidetracked at this point. Some groups, at this stage, have become "addicted" to research and information-gathering and have a hard

---

The Citizens Clearinghouse for Hazardous Waste, Box 296, Arlington, VA 22216 (703/276-7070) helps leaders in over 500 communities fight hazardous waste problems. This article, by Lois Marie Gibbs and Will Collette, is excerpted with permission from Engage/Social Action, *October 1984.*

time moving into action until "we collect just a little more information." Other groups decide that what they should do is hire a lawyer to solve the problem—a choice that is, at best, expensive and time-consuming, and, at worst, a disaster as the group stops building its political power on the hope that now the lawyer will solve the problem for them. Other groups decide to let local politicians do the work for them, falling for such smooth lines as, "I'm glad you brought this to my attention; I share your concern and I'll get right to it." This pitfall has caused many tragedies.

The two main sources of power in our communities are money and people. Since most of us do not have money, *we must rely on our people.* Never lose sight of that fact. Whenever your group sits together to discuss what needs to be done, a central question should always be: "Are we making the best and most effective use of our people power?"

Your actions from this point forward should focus on winning a successful resolution of the issue that caused you to come together. At this stage, most groups served by CCHW will call a meeting with government officials and industry people pinpointed as "targets" because they have the *power* to grant people what they need.

Tactics should contain an element of fun. Because organizing is so hard, make every effort to make sure people enjoy doing it. Don't go empty-handed. Though most groups bring flyers, fact sheets or picket signs, other props can help get your message across.

Incorporate your community churches into your actions. Some groups use religious services as part of all the action! For example, if your issue includes waste dumptrucks cruising through your neighborhood, how about a church service right in the middle of the road!

We have a long way to go. We must find solutions that are more than just having hazardous waste taken "somewhere else." While we have the right to fight for our communities, we must also fight for *all* communities, since what is an injustice for anyone of us is an injustice for all of us.

THE SEARCH FOR A NEW BOWL AND SALT

by James N. Brewster

The people of the city [Jericho] said to Elisha, "You can see how pleasantly our city is situated, but the water is polluted, and the country is troubled by miscarriages." He said, "Fetch me a new bowl and put some salt in it." When they had fetched it, he went out to the spring and, throwing the salt into it, he said, "This is the Word of the Lord: 'I purify this water. It shall cause no more death or miscarriage.'" The water remained pure till this day, in fulfillment of Elisha's word.
2 Kings 2:19-22 (New English Bible)

This old and very simple story of Elisha's first miracle in his public ministry at the well in Jericho is the stuff which frames my problems of pollution, too. Just as I was thinking that the crisis of Love Canal was a contemporary predicament, Elisha, the bald-headed prophet, entered and spoke directly to me from almost three thousand years ago.

Like the people of Jericho, we have built our cities in "pleasant" places. They are places filled with promise, places where we hope our real estate values will increase, where our children have good schooling and we live in relative safety.

We want to dwell "forever" in these pleasant places— from the Native Americans looking for the right place for their portable villages to the white settlers looking for the ideal location to build their cabins. I respond favorably to this desire. It is part of our history. We want to leave behind the places of our past. Move up! Or out! Live in a better area, or a finer neighborhood.

Niagara Falls was one of those places.

Walt Whitman, the 19th century poet, described the day in 1880 when he first saw the Falls:

For really seizing a great picture or book, or piece of music...or grand scenery...there comes some lucky five minutes of a man's life... The present case about two o'clock this afternoon, gave me Niagara, its superb severity of action and color and majestic grouping, in one short, indescribable show. We were very slowly crossing the suspension bridge—the day clear, sunny, still— and I out on the platform. The Falls were in plain view about a mile off. The river tumbling green and white, far below me: the dark high banks...brief, and as quiet as brief, that picture—a remembrance always afterwards. Such are the things, indeed, I lay away with my life's rare and blessed bits of hours.

I can understand Whitman's enthusiasm. Not long ago, very early one morning, my mind already noisy with the day's schedule, I left the house, and as I opened the car door in the backyard, I heard the roaring of the Falls. A mile distant. Yet I felt that moment of poetry which lifted me beyond the blaring of my own business to hear the deeper Sound. "A pleasant situation," indeed.

And I am sure that the new residents of Love Canal shared those feelings in the 1950's, when they responded to advertisements like these in the local paper:

Homes are replacing strawberry patches. Clean, fresh country air, but still within the city. It's to your advantage to inquire...now. Home increase due to wage increase is expected immediately. Protect yourself on today's prices and save.

Lots across the street from the Canal were described in 1960 as "nice residential." An ad for renters stressed that "children (are) welcome in these brand-new three bedroom ranch-type units...with spacious yards."

Why move to Jericho? For the same things which Whitman saw in Niagara Falls. Or for the same reasons which prompted people to move into the new houses at Love Canal. Yet, having made our decision, we have, like the residents of Jericho, discovered trouble in the Promised Land.

The people of Jericho spoke of their disillusionment: "Our city is pleasantly situated, *but the water is polluted...*"

A bulldozer operator from Niagara Falls describes his work at Love Canal before the land was purchased for development:

They would bring me truckloads of chemicals. There are phosphorous compounds in there. They used to blow up every day. There are sodium compounds in there. They used to bring the chemicals in drums, in powdered form, in cakes,

---

From a sermon by James N. Brewster, minister of St. Paul's United Methodist Church, Niagara Falls, NY.

and dump them. The canal was fifteen feet deep in some places, twenty in other places and twenty-five in other places. After we started to fill in the canal, in the morning when we would begin we would find between twenty and thirty dead sea gulls each day. That was about thirty years ago. I saw a dog swim across the canal and when it got to the other side, it dropped dead. One day, I stepped in some of the contaminated soil. I took the shoes off that night that had the gook on them. The next morning when I got up and looked for the shoes, I found nothing left but the heels and the soles.

In some versions of the Scripture from 2 Kings, "miscarriages" are not the word used to describe a result of the water pollution. The Revised Standard Version states that the "land is unfruitful." In either case, the meaning is clear. Creation is troubled by water which is not pure.

Some Old Testament scholars question whether there was a connection between the pollution of the well in Jericho and the miscarriages. Yet this was not questioned by the residents of Jericho. Nor, for the most part, do we question it.

Luella Kenny, a former resident of Love Canal, submitted this testimony in 1983 before a Joint Public Hearing on Future Uses of the Love Canal Hazardous Waste Site and Adjacent Property:

In 1969, my husband and I purchased a home on 96th and Greenwald Avenue, one-tenth of a mile from the northern perimeter of Love Canal. The home had about one acre of land. The property was bounded by the 93rd Street School playground and the junction of Bergholtz, Cayuga and Black Creeks. An outfall that drained the sewers in the northern section of Love Canal emptied into Black Creek at this juncture in our yard.

We had three sons, the last of which was born while we lived in Love Canal. The three boys enjoyed playing in the yard and in the creek area. In June, 1978, our youngest son became ill. He was diagnosed as having nephrosis, a disease of the kidneys, whereby protein is excreted into the urine and fluid is retained. We were told not to worry because it could be treated and Jon would outgrow this disease by the time he was fourteen... to quote the pediatric urologist, "It's the best disease a child can have, so don't worry about him."

Four months later, Jon was dead.

Elisha's response to the problems of pollution at the well in Jericho was immediate and positive. He sent for a new bowl and salt, poured the salt into the well, and the problem was resolved.

This was extraordinary. Elisha knew the remedy *before* even seeing the well! And here lies the difference between the well at Jericho and our poisoned groundwater. Today, we have no "Elisha's Miraculous Monumental Mixture." We live in a world in which pollution is caused by the improper disposal of chemicals like benzene, toluene, trichlorophenol, hexachlorocyclohexane and octachlorocyclopentene (C-58). Contamination is measured in parts per billion (equivalent to one second in thirty-two years), or parts per trillion (one second in thirty-two thousand years).

I imagine a modern day Elisha (now called a "consultant") being called in by a committee from Times Beach, Missouri. They complain, "Our town is a pleasant place to live, but the place is polluted and people are sick." Today's Elisha would have no quick answer, though. He would have to go roaming about town, poking through attics, listening to people in laboratories and workshops, trying to find the twentieth century equivalent of the salt and the new bowl.

Love Canal Update: How the Churches Responded

It has been six years since Love Canal became a household word.

What has happened since that time?

The once-residential area is now a fenced-off ghost town. Clean-up efforts have been underway since 1978. Medical studies give differing reports on damage to health and chromosomes. Some settlement has been made to the former residents.

Now there's another twist: The toxic wastes that were taken from the Love Canal area and put into the Cecos International landfill near Niagara Falls may themselves be leaking out. According to an investigator from the Environmental Protection Agency, these wastes, along with "materials" from a DuPont Company disposal site nearby, may be endangering people living just downstream.

Cecos International, a subsidiary of Browning-Ferris Industries, is one of the largest waste dumps in the country, and supposedly secure, so it has received wastes from many other "deficient" sites through the federal government's "Superfund" law. Is it now deficient too? One EPA official states that the EPA has known for a long time that there are problems with the Cecos site, but, "We're running out of sites to send the wastes to." Eventually, he said, the disposal of hazardous wastes in landfills will be barred. "Industry is headed in that direction already."

In the meantime, how can Christians respond to such abuse of God's earth? James Brewster reflects on how the churches aided Love Canal victims when other systems failed.

In natural disasters, volunteer organizations customarily provide important assistance for the victims. In the Niagara Falls metropolitan area, not one traditionally helping group, except the church, responded to the Love Canal people. There was no rallying of Boy Scouts, Lions Club or Rotary.

In natural disasters, whole communities are often strengthened and drawn together with a positive public spirit as they aid the victims. But Love Canal resulted in a collapse of supportive structures. Victims were isolated from the community. No local politician championed their cause. Doctors were reluctant to treat them. The sanctuary found in the safety of the home was severely threatened. Two neighborhood schools were shut down almost at the outset. Wesley United Methodist Church valiantly ministered in the community until July 1981 and then was closed.

Alienated from the larger community, the people complained bitterly of a lack of faith and trust in government to fulfill its constitutional obligations regarding the health and safety of the citizens. The announcement "I'm from the government; I'm here to help" became a warning signal rather than a sign of genuine aid. To outsiders, the words "Love Canal" meant the terror of toxic landfills; for those living in the area, it suggested despair and helplessness resulting from government ineptness. The disaster was obviously chemical, but it was also institutional.

Counseling was put to the extreme test. Answering the victims' questions was critical: "How does this chemical affect my health?" "Shall I move or stay?" "Is it all right for us to have children?" A ministry reaching beyond "band-aid" treatment was imperative. Given such injustice, the churches are drawn into strategies which include legal action on behalf of the victims when political solutions are inadequate or nonexistent.

Given the enormity of the problems relating to hazardous waste still beneath the surface—the federal government has listed 53,000 toxic waste sites in the United States—how can the church respond? It has neither the willingness nor the resources to deal with all these potential nonnatural disasters.

It is urgent that the ecumenical community respond *strategically* to certain major problem areas now. An official of the U.S. Environmental Protection Agency's hazardous waste control division has asked religious groups to adopt "pressure point tactics," giving priority to cases that will set national precedent and therefore will affect how legislation, regulation, courts and corporations are to deal with countless other Love Canals. The EPA official states that church-related agencies may be the *only* institutions in the country possessing the power and tenacity to resolve a number of the important problems about toxic and hazardous wastes. Unlike citizen groups and homeowners' associations, whose activities are largely self-serving and short-term, the religious groups have an integrity and a selfless motivation that can exert important leverage in the political arena and the courts.

Such encouragement and support by church-related agencies offer some hope for the victims of nonnatural disasters.

— *James N. Brewster*

Copyright 1982, Christian Century Foundation. Reprinted by permission from the August 4–11, 1982 issue of The Christian Century.

Lifestyle	Emission Controls	Authorities	join a citizens group	FOOD	trade restrictions
drinking water	Government	DAMS	Prevention	drinking water supply and sanitation decade	HEALTH
Children	sanitation facility in each settlement	Animals	free international trade	Consumption	EXPERTS
Pollution	ENERGY	land reclamation	Regulations	LAND	hazardous waste spill
Pesticides	value all cultures	Cooperation	food self-sufficiency	Barriers	Individual
CHANGE	Obsolete	United Nations	Recycling	POVERTY	eat lower on the food chain

WEALTH	HUNGER	Education	right to food	Science	write to a member of Congress
small scale farms	LAW	solar energy for homes	CHURCH	ACID RAIN	Politics
Planning	well in each settlement	Competition	MEN	Technology	Grain Reserves
reduced population growth	Employment	raw sewage	Democracy	trade restrictions	ENOUGH
SMALL SCALE	AIR	Partnership	participation in decision making	DAMS	WATER SPORTS
JUSTICE	appropriate technology	WOMEN	Conservation	HAND PUMPS	WATER

AFTER THE URANIUM SPILL...
A Navajo Community Takes Stock
by Barbara H. Chase

That hot, dry, dusty July 16th morning in 1979 gave no clue that it would become a day to remember. The clear blue New Mexico sky offered no evidence that the day would mark the beginning of dark forebodings. Farmers with livestock, mostly sheep, assumed that the water in the Rio Puerco would be sufficient for watering, as usual.

Some people said the Navajos had no right to use the Rio Puerco (that typical western stream which zigzags across Arizona and New Mexico) or the washes as a watering hole, but the mining company upriver had never forbidden its use. The United Nuclear Mining Corporation was on private land and the Navajo community of Church Rock was adjacent to it.

Those who worked at the United Nuclear Mining Corporation were preparing to go to work as usual — all except those who had been aroused during the night by the disaster that would eventually affect them all.

The news came to the Navajos at Church Rock that an earthen dam upriver had broken and some kind of liquid waste had come rushing through and down into the Rio Puerco. At the time, who could comprehend the implications?

The first newspaper reports indicated that 325 million gallons of radioactive water had breached the dam (*Gallup Independent,* July 17, 1979), but later it was ascertained that *only* 94 million gallons had broken through! This is the largest such spill to occur in a uranium mill in all the United States!

While the mill was immediately shut down, much needed to be done to determine the extent of the damage to land, human beings and animals. That determination remains a question to many who live and work and make their livelihood in that area of the country.

When the New Mexico Environmental Improvement Division (NMEID) closed the mill, they also began sampling soil and water in cooperation with the Nuclear Regulatory Commission (NRC).

The United Nuclear Corporation (UNC) immediately

This material has been excerpted from the larger study: Walking in Harmony: The Earth, Sky, Water, People, *by Barbara H. Chase, published by the New Mexico Council of Churches, 1984. The study is available from the NMCC, 124 Hermosa, S.E. Albuquerque, NM 87108 at $4.00 per copy.*

began repairing the dam and by 7:40 a.m. on the day of the spill, the flow from the uranium mill pond was stopped.

The NMEID suggested that the water of the Rio Puerco not be used. Signs were put up in the river beds in English, Spanish and Navajo stating: "All use of water from this river is discouraged by the NMEID."

No lives were lost (directly attributable to the spill) and immediate danger to the people and livestock living near the Rio Puerco was presumed to be limited.

The newspapers dutifully reported on the spill as well. As one reads the accounts it is easy to understand the rising fear and anxiety of those living near the Rio Puerco. The Rio Puerco, which had been a friend, which had shared its water with the sheep, the other livestock, the people, was now a "danger" — or might be! What the "danger" was, was not clear. For how long it would be "dangerous," no one could tell the people. The difference between "serious" and "dangerous" was never explained.

LOCAL PEOPLE TAKE ACTION
About a week after the spill, the Church Rock Chapter organized an Action Committee. It sought to inform the people about what was going on, as well as to assess how people's special needs could be met.

One of the first needs was for clean water. Some families in the area had as many as 400 head of sheep and some cows, which would mean hauling about 400 gallons of water a day plus that which was needed for human consumption. Helen George, secretary of the Church Rock Action Committee, indicated in an interview with a Church World Service official that the people also anticipated having to buy grain and feed because of the contamination. When the dam breached and spilled its contents into the Puerco Wash the grazing areas had been cut off. The people were afraid to take their cattle through the wash to get to the other side.

In August, six Navajos (five children and one adult) who might have come into contact with radioactive puddles were tested at the Los Alamos Scientific Laboratory. This was done as a precautionary measure; no illness had been noted. LANL reported within a few days that there were no apparent health defects but the entire story would not be known until the Center for Disease Control report was in. After months of waiting it revealed that the level of radioactivity in each person was normal.

While the Church Rock people were anxious about the spill, the United Nuclear Corporation was trying to clean it up while at the same time negotiating with all the necessary agencies to reopen the mill. With the high unemployment in the area the closing of the mill was a continuing hardship and by October 1979 the UNC felt it was time to reopen. On October 27, 1979, 15 weeks after the spill, the UNC mill reopened. For the unemployed workers and the industry, it was a good day—but for many there were simply still too many unanswered questions.

After reopening in October 1979, UNC did some reorganization and hired new staff, seeking people with sensitivity to the local community and commitment to better community relations. But in 1982, after suffering a series of misfortunes, complex problems with regulatory agencies and the depression of the uranium industry, UND decided to close.

"The story" might now be said to have been told. The bare facts, with a few editorial notes and reflections, have been laid before you. But as there seems to be difficulty in pinpointing an exact beginning to the story, no specific date can be given to say "it is ended." The story of people affected by the spill will never end for those families most deeply affected physically, spiritually and psychologically. The industry will continue to be a part of the story as it seeks ways to continue its business, tackle legal suits and the demands of local, state and federal agencies.

The event, the disaster occurred.

WHAT ARE THE IMPLICATIONS OF THIS TECHNOLOGICAL DISASTER?

The background setting is the uranium mills tailing spill at Church Rock, New Mexico, but the implications are to be found — is it too much to say? — almost everywhere. The disaster is classified as a technological disaster, in contrast to a *natural* disaster. And while it would be comforting to believe that similar technological disasters cannot happen, or will now happen less often, the reports seem to indicate just the opposite.

As we become more sophisticated and more "advanced" in the development and use of technology, the need to monitor safety precautions, to establish standards and regulations, to measure the environmental as well as the human and spiritual impact is increasingly important and vital to each of us for mere survival.

In the case of the technological disaster at Church Rock, a group of concerned persons from the Christian community began to feel they should become involved in some meaningful ministry. With assistance from the National Council of Churches of Christ in the U.S.A., a Rio Puerco Coordinating Committee was established under the auspices of the New Mexico Conference of Churches. The committee brought together concerned pastors, officials of the Indian Health Service located at Window Rock, Arizona, (headquarters of the Navajo Protection Commission) to find the best way to be of assistance to the Navajo community. Few in the group had much experience in the area of technological disasters. Nor had anyone spent much time exploring the theological dimensions of such involvement. The lay participants from Window Rock had the best understanding of the implications, yet even they felt somewhat helpless to get at the fears and anxieties of the people affected.

But the commitment to involvement was there and the group set out on the journey. Today, the members feel their experiences are worth sharing. It has become obvious that such technological disasters will continue and that concerned persons, particularly those with a sense of the sacredness of God's creation, need to prepare for them.

The story as you have just read it might be said to be the heart of the disaster which occurred that July day in 1979. It certainly was not the beginning. When did the disaster first begin? Was it when uranium was first discovered (or created)? Was it when someone learned to mine it? Or when it was discovered that it was a key mineral for making nuclear bombs and useful as an energy resource? Or was it when it was decided (by whom?) that stockpiling nuclear armaments was the way to peace? Do we look to the miners, to the managers, or to the regulators? The precise beginning may never be known to us since so many factors are involved. So we must deal with the present and try to prevent such disasters from occurring in the future.

How Churches Can Respond to Non-natural Disasters

This country could be facing some of the most insidious disasters in its history: disasters that could affect every state, many communities and thousands of men, women and children. They have to do with the transportation of hazardous material, nuclear accidents, toxic waste.

Churches need to team up with government and private agencies to help eliminate these hazards and yet be prepared to cope with any situation that occurs in their community.

While each church should have a plan, churches working together will have far more impact. The church has many resources and capacities. They can be the instigators of action and their resources are oftentimes supplemental to local government and private disaster agencies.

PREPAREDNESS

Where Civil Defense and Red Cross preparedness plans exist, churches may become a vital part of their program by making their facilities available as shelters, feeding and first-aid stations, day nurseries, etc.

Most preparedness plans provide for emergency food, clothing, shelter and medical aid to persons affected by disaster. Tornadoes, floods and other "natural" disasters were at one time the chief concern. Today, communities should be ready to handle evacuees from danger areas caused by transportation or nuclear accidents or toxic waste.

Denominations and councils may want to survey local churches to discover where available volunteers are and what skills they have; facilities offered for shelters and other services; vehicles available for transportation; as well as other items that would be helpful to know in an emergency situation.

PASTORAL CARE

In situations where toxic waste or nuclear accidents necessitate evacuating people or even create anxiety due to the threat of the unknown, pastors and qualified laypersons perform the churches' most important role of pastoral care. These persons should be well-versed on the problems of pyschological and physical distress and resources available to cope with the effects of these types of disasters.

For more information, contact the Church World Service Domestic Disaster Office, Box 188, New Windsor, MD 21776. Tel: (301) 635-6464 (Ext. 125).

ADVOCACY

Love Canal, for example, has an ecumenical task force made up of several denominations that have been very effective in acting as the advocate for the families affected by chemical waste.

They are the pioneers and are a model for action for churches in other communities who will be affected by toxic waste.

There are several important advocacy roles the church can assume. One is to direct the persons affected by the disaster to the right resource and act on their behalf to see that their total needs are met through government, private agencies and churches.

Another is to take an active part in community affairs that relate to controls, safety precautions, and elimination of hazards.

Still another would be to use the church as a medium for distribution of facts available through the League of Women Voters Educational Fund, Environmental Protection Agency, Department of Transportation and local and state agencies and coalitions formed locally to cope with hazardous waste.

RESEARCH AND ANALYSIS

Research and analysis is a top priority item in both the private and government sectors.

The League of Women Voters Educational Fund is to be commended for the excellent job they are doing in cooperation with the American Public Health Association, the Environmental Action Foundation, the Ezaak Walton League of America, The National Wildlife Federation and the Technical Information Project, all of the private sector.

The United States Environmental Protection Agency, Solid Waste Division and Superfund are a group of people who are sincerely dedicated to coping with this serious situation.

"Waste Alert" is a federally sponsored program, coordinated by the American Public Health Association and designed to bring citizens up-to-date on pollution and involve them in solving the waste problem. Watch for scheduled meetings of "Waste Alert" in your area.

MITIGATION

Toxic waste must be dumped somewhere until science discovers a better way to dispose of it. Therefore, mitigation becomes important. When it is decided that industry may put toxic waste in your community, take an active role in choosing the facilities. Be alert to health and environmental concerns resulting from disposal sites; be knowledgeable about the environmental factors which might influence disposal sites. . . for additional information on these and other questions, write to the U.S. Environmental Protection Agency, Office of Public Awareness (A-107), Washington, D.C. 20460.

HOW TO MAKE HARD DECISIONS ABOUT ENERGY

Creating a just energy policy is difficult because inevitably, some ethically desirable goals must be "traded off" against other goals which are also good. Precisely because such decisions are not simple, they should be made only after maximum public consideration, with conscious awareness of what good goals are being sacrificed, and agreement that the sacrifice is necessary. The ethic of ecological justice indicates some general guidelines which should apply when decisions are being made about energy policy:

1. If using a technology poses a risk of irreversible global damage, great prudence and caution should be exercised in deciding about its use. The greater the risk, the less moral justification there is for its use.
2. The survival needs of those who are below the minimum material standard of living should be met before the wants of those above that standard. Since survival depends on energy, it should be distributed by a standard that insures adequate food, health, housing, and clean air and water for all.
3. The views of those who will be affected by a particular action should be heard in the decision-making process.
4. The effect on future generations of today's decisions must be considered.
5. Those who receive the benefits of energy decisions should, as much as possible, bear the costs.
6. Regardless of their size or political influence, all countries should have access to full and responsible participation in arenas in which research and policy decisions are made which will affect their energy futures.
7. Quality of life considerations — such as human dignity, satisfaction in employment, community cohesion and religion — must be considered along with technical and economic factors.

From "The Ethical Implications of Energy Production and Use," adopted by the Governing Board of the National Council of Churches of Christ in the U.S.A., May, 1979.

"...The Fullness Thereof"
Caring for Our Common Heritage

"The earth is the Lord's and the fullness thereof..." sang the Psalmist. Human beings have always felt the challenge to probe the depths of the unexplored—the sea and the rainforests, the moon and planets have always challenged us. In light of their understanding of the gospel and their recognition that the world's resources are so unevenly distributed among the earth's peoples, many Christians are saying that the untapped resources of the universe are for all to share. Among these gifts of God are air, water, the vast genetic variety of plants and animals, Antarctica, the moon and planets and outer space...all of which are now threatened by human exploitation, pollution and even by plans for warfare. "Common heritage" is the term used to describe cooperation in caring for these resources. The United Methodist Church is among the churches that support international efforts towards the Law of the Sea Treaty and the Agreement Governing the Activities of States on the Moon and Other Celestial Bodies. Political agreements are necessary; but people of faith also recognize that we have a responsibility as God's people to use what God has given us to benefit all the world's people.

Adapted from The Book of Resolutions, *United Methodist Church.*

A VISION OF LIFE IN ALL ITS FULLNESS

*...let justice roll down like waters,
and righteousness like an everflowing stream.
(Amos 5:24)*

THE SEARCH FOR A NEW HUMILITY

by William E. Gibson

I am the Lord your God from the land of Egypt;
you know no God but me, and besides me there is no savior.
It was I who knew you in the wilderness, in the land of drought;
but when they had fed to the full, they were filled,
  and their heart was lifted up; therefore they forgot me.
So I will be to them like a lion, like a leopard I will lurk beside the way.
I will fall upon them like a bear robbed of her cubs... (Hosea 13:4-8)

When Hosea addressed the situation of the last corrupt, chaotic years of the northern kingdom, he announced, "The Lord has a controversy with the inhabitants of the land." It was the controversy of a caring God with a people who had turned away. "There is no faithfulness or kindness," said the prophet, "and no knowledge of God in the land." (Hosea 4:1)

> *The economic forces which move [modern industry] are hardly qualified at a single point by really ethical considerations. If, while it is in the flush of its early triumphs, it may seem impossible to bring it under the restraint of moral law, it may strengthen faith to know that life without law destroys itself. If the church can do nothing else, it can bear witness to the truth until such a day as bitter experience will force a recalcitrant civilization to a humility which it does not now possess.*

These words were written more than half a century ago by the theologian Reinhold Niebuhr as he packed his bags and prepared to leave a parish in industrial Detroit for Union Theological Seminary. It was the last entry in the journal that would be published as *Leaves From the Notebook of a Tamed Cynic.*

At the time Niebuhr left Detroit, the automobile industry epitomized the dynamism of the American economy as it triumphantly attained levels of production so dazzling that they turned America into a consumer society and became the model for the world.

I think that now in the 1980's we may better understand what Niebuhr said in 1928. This paper will build on the last sentence of Niebuhr's journal to offer a broad analysis of contemporary realities, an analysis that is infused continuously with insights from the biblical story as it is found in the Book of Hosea.

BITTER EXPERIENCE

In the flush of the triumphs of industrial civilization, it was virtually impossible to stem the tide of devotion and commitment to economic growth and material abundance. A few voices were raised against the unjust dehumanizing consequences of greed and acquisitiveness. Nevertheless, the application of science-based technology to industry seemed so marvelously successful, that most people were willing to put up with the competition, the viciousness, the boredom, the hierarchical organization and the inequalities. It seemed that we were moving steadily toward a time when just about everybody could and would be rich.

Then, beginning in the mid-1960's and reaching a kind of climax in 1980, came mounting evidence that something was fundamentally wrong. The ranks of the world's poor were swelling, even as the heights of affluence kept rising for the privileged. Natural resources were disappearing and natural systems were deteriorating in direct proportion to the expansion of production and consumption. The track on which the modern world was driving seemed to be carrying it towards a suicidal crash.

Friends, the evidence is massive; the crisis is real. The warnings began to come even during the booming progress of the Eisenhower-Kennedy-Johnson era. Michael Harrington wrote *The Other America*; Rachel Carson, *Silent Spring*; Paul Ehrlich, *The Population Bomb.*

The war on poverty, however, took it for granted that

William E. Gibson is coordinator of the Eco-Justice Project, Center for Religion, Ethics and Social Policy, Ithaca, NY.

This article was originally a presentation to two of the Social Ministry Institutes sponsored by the Program Agency of The Presbyterian Church (U.S.A.). It was originally published by the Center for Religion, Ethics and Social Policy.

the conquest of poverty could be achieved through economic growth based upon the conquest of nature by science, technology and industry. This was the national consensus.

In the riots of the 60's black people expressed frustration at systematic exclusion from sharing fairly in a constantly growing economic "pie." Their gains in that period, hard-won and limited as they were, were based on that consensus. But by 1970, voices were raised to suggest that the pie could not keep on growing—or that if it did, the results might not be beneficial.

That was the year of the first Earth Day. In 1972, a landmark book, *The Limits to Growth,* warned that a continuation of present trends in population, industrialization, food production, pollution, and resource depletion would lead to overshoot and collapse sometime in the coming century. By the end of the decade, the literature of what I call the "eco-justice crisis" had become voluminous. Herman Daly was the spokesman for steady-state economics; E. F. Schumacher, the advocate of human-scale, non-violent technology.

In 1980 the warnings became official. By that, I mean that they came from the government of the United States. *The Global 2000 Report to the President* was important, not because it said anything new, but because it came from the Department of State and the Council on Environmental Quality. The first sentence of the report is the one most quoted: "If present trends continue, the world in 2000 will be more crowded, more polluted, less stable ecologically, and more vulnerable to disruption than the one we live in now." It quickly went on to say that conditions would not be better for hundreds of millions of the desperately poor, and that for many they would be worse, "unless the nations of the world act decisively to alter current trends."

Two other reports in the same year helped to lay out for the public and for public officials the dimensions of the crisis. *North-South: A Program for Survival* came from the Independent Commission on International Development Issues, chaired by Willy Brandt, former Chancellor of West Germany. This report pointed immediately to the growing gap between rich and poor countries. It called for a North-South dialogue and concerted global action "to give every society a full opportunity to...satisfy the essential needs of its people at an acceptable pace."

Finally, the report of the Presidential Commission on World Hunger called on the U.S. Government to "make the elimination of hunger the primary focus of its relations with the developing countries, beginning with the decade of the 1980s." The motivation for action, according to the report, is not only a sense of responsibility to alleviate suffering and correct inequity, but also a realization that we *had better* act, because our own national security is endangered by mounting chaos and conflict and even the growing possibility of nuclear war.

THE LORD'S CONTROVERSY WITH US

If we read the three reports of 1980 in the context of the biblical story, they become, not simply a secular message about newly recognized dangers, but rather the bill of particulars for the Lord's controversy with us. They become the detailed evidence of the faithlessness inherent in the main thrust of Western civilization and in the life goals and daily habits of all who pursue wealth and power by forsaking the righteousness and steadfast love that constitute the faithfulness of a covenant relationship with God.

> *A trader, in whose hands are false balances, [Ephraim] loves to oppress. Ephraim has said, Ah, but I am rich, I have gained wealth for myself; but all his riches can never offset the guilt he has incurred. (Hosea 12:7 f)*

Hosea's report and the three reports of 1980 present details of the oppression of the poor. In Hosea's time and in our own time, wealthy individuals or nations protect and magnify their wealth—they keep it, they do not share it; and they increase it, usually by taking advantage of the poor. The difference between Hosea's time and our time is that in our modern world the technical means are available to overcome poverty and hunger.

The three reports of 1980 also present the details of the oppression of the earth. The care of creation has degenerated into conquest and domination. Western culture has lost the sense of the divinely imputed value of all that is.

The difference between Hosea's time and our time is the immense amount of damage people today can do—in the scale and speed of environmental deterioration and resource depletion due to violent technology, overconsumption, wastefulness and the population explosion. The connection between the ecological reality and the overcoming of poverty is that, with all our scientific progress, we do *not* have the technical means to overcome poverty *unless* we respect the earth's limits and the generations still unborn, and learn to share equitably the good things of God's creation. Meanwhile, the lament of the land sounds more appropriate to our time than to Hosea's:

> *...the land mourns, and all who dwell in it languish, and also the beasts of the field, and the birds of the air; and even the fish of the sea are taken away. (Hosea 4:3)*

The bitter experience is now at hand. As Niebuhr said many times, "the law of life is love." Because he saw that the economic forces that move American industry were hardly qualified by considerations of love as fairness or as insistence on the common good, he knew that a time of troubles lay ahead. The "bottom line" was growth and profit. Other considerations—job security, safety, the needs of people who lack effective demand, environmental protection, and resource conservation—were accepted willingly *only* if they made a positive impact on the bottom-line, and resisted determinedly if they did not.

Langdon Gilkey, in a 1981 article in *The Christian Century,* writes perceptively about present troubles. He sees two main indications of the breakdown and transformation of our culture. The first is the ecological crisis. Unless there is a radical transformation of the "technological, industrial establishment," our culture, he says, "has a very good chance of destroying itself through increasingly inadequate supplies, through endless conflicts for those ever scantier materials, and through the systems of control and authority necessary to cope with each of these dangers."

This represents bitter experience indeed, because the problem is "essential and not accidental." It arises precisely from our culture's successes and creativity with respect to science, technology, and material abundance! Suddenly, those successes have become ever harder to sustain.

The second threatening indication of change, says Gilkey, is "the dramatic shift in the past few decades in the relative power and influence of [western] culture." Although European countries have begun to adjust to this, "America...has yet even to try to realize that domination is no longer a possibility or a possible goal, that world power must be shared... [even] with groups holding quite other cultural and value systems...." This change in America's position of influence, says Gilkey, "is felt every day by Americans; and it is expressed by them in a wide variety of frustrated, angry, anxious and 'macho' ways." This, too, is bitter experience. The image that we have cherished of our country and its role in the world, not only as dominant but as *righteous,* is being shattered; and this is painful to accept. We have lost both our position and our innocence, and we do not like it.

> *The pride of Israel witnesses against him... Israel has forgotten his maker, and built palaces; and Judah has multiplied fortified cities; but I will send a fire upon his cities, and it shall devour his strongholds. Rejoice not, O Israel!...for you have played the harlot, forsaking your God. (Hosea 7:10, 8:14, 9:1)*

A RECALCITRANT CIVILIZATION

It would be an understatement to suggest that the government is now ignoring the three reports. To the contrary, its policies constitute an official and emphatic repudiation of them and all the warnings they contain.

The cornerstone of policy is now an ideological rededication to economic growth without limit or regulation. Let business, specifically *big* business, be unshackled. Let profits rise by taxing corporations less; let depreciation of capital stock accelerate; let us have new plants, more bigness, greater centralization. Let us insist that this can come to pass despite our still-precarious dependence on fossil fuels.

The Reagan Administration virtually dismantled the Council on Environmental Quality and seriously crippled the Environmental Protection Agency.

In response to the chief recommendation of the Presidential Commission on World Hunger, that the U.S. make overcoming hunger the primary focus of its relations with developing countries, the administration and the Congress shifted the emphasis in U.S. aid from development to "security." Development assistance cuts helped to increase military aid and political support for shaky third world regimes. Contributions to U.N. and multilateral development programs were reduced.

In response to the call of the North-South Report for bold, vigorous new international cooperation to reduce the gap between rich and poor countries, the President went to Cancun in 1981 and told the delegates to the summit meeting that they must depend on "free enterprise." He did not show any understanding that the kind of free enterprise that has prevailed in global development has widened the rich-poor gap, both within and between nations. Free enterprise by itself cannot fundamentally reallocate access to resources or redistribute incomes or power. It responds to the market demand and investment decisions of those who already have more than enough rather than to the real but ineffective demand of the poor who need and lack the basic essentials for survival.

I believe that the government's policies are now so contradictory to the fundamental realities and requirements of our time that they can work in the short run, if at all, only by an intensifying assault on the earth and the poor and by enormously exacerbating the world's problems in the slightly longer run.

I really do not mean just to "dump" on Mr. Reagan and blame him for everything that alarms me about present policy. I see him as the authentic spokesman for a large and powerful segment of the American people. These people want desperately to deny that there are limits to growth and consumerism, and that the present economic order is both unjust and unsustainable. They want, also, to deny the evidence that casts doubt on the power of the United States to remain Number One in the world. And certainly they cannot entertain the idea that it may not be good for the world to be dominated by us.

> Like a stubborn heifer, Israel is stubborn; can the Lord now feed them like a lamb in a broad pasture? (Hosea 4:16)

BEARING WITNESS TO THE TRUTH

When the prophet says, "There is no faithfulness or kindness, and no knowledge of God in the land," he brings together three aspects of one behavior. There is no knowledge of God precisely because there is no faithfulness or kindness. Instead, there is "lying, killing, stealing, and committing adultery."

What then does it mean to convey the knowledge of God in the midst of the eco-justice crisis? We must not speak glibly about knowing God. Nevertheless, the biblical story requires us to believe that the God of steadfast love is doing and saying something which may be quite new, in and through the realities and events of our own time.

Surely the Lord has a controversy with the inhabitants of *this* land. The bitter experience comes now and will intensify. The bitter experience is the judgment of God, seeking to bring a recalcitrant civilization to a humility it does not now possess:

> So you, by the help of your God, return, hold fast to love and justice, and wait continually for your God. (Hosea 12:6)

Bearing witness to the truth means illuminating the present crises so that they can be understood as the Lord's controversy with this nation, a controversy that God presses particularly with those who belong to the church and who therefore profess to be God's people. We illuminate the present crisis by taking all the information we can get about conditions and events, and by the light from the biblical story, interpreting them in terms of God's steadfast loving purpose for persons and nations.

Bearing witness to the truth means explaining the crisis of our time—explaining it so that people can discern within it the work of God in judgment and deliverance, and so that people can see the bitter experience as the consequence of injustice and faithlessness.

People need to know about the realities of poverty and hunger and their roots in unjust, cruel systems that operate to reward the greedy and to encourage the carelessness of the comfortable. They need to know that God's created order imposes limits on human behavior. They need to know that prosperity that depends on devouring scarce resources, abusing natural systems and exploiting cheap labor is both unjust and suicidal. They need to see that justice in the sense of a sustainable sufficiency for all depends upon creating new institutions and mechanisms, domestic and international, for sharing access to the natural and human resources necessary for life.

Witness to the truth occurs in many forms: in preaching; in teaching; in prayer and liturgy; in pastoral concern for those who are threatened by the truth; in study, advocacy, and action to find new economic and political alternatives; and in joining hands with others to seek abundance, not in things that we could do without, but in good work, loving community, and a new covenant of faithfulness.

In seeking to bear witness to the truth, we take the risk in faith that we can be instruments of the knowledge of God. An awesome task at any time, it is doubly so at this major turning point in history. If ever the task could be shaken, the time is not now, when the quality and the very continuation of life on this planet hang precariously in the balance. This is not the time for casual Christianity or business-as-usual in the church. It is a time for special sensitivity and, very likely, for special courage.

THE FRUITS OF A NEW HUMILITY
Niebuhr suggested that bitter experience would force a recalcitrant civilization to a new humility. But he surely meant, also, that the church's interpretation of the bitter experience might itself be instrumental to the new humility.

If we learn to read with compassion the cold statistics of wretchedness and starvation and to feel the shame and outrage of this unnecessary violation of the solidarity of the human family, that is grace. If we hear with similar concern the implication of present trends for children not yet born, that is grace. If we acknowledge not only the limitations of science and technology, but also the violence and abuse that have been associated with their use in Western culture, that is grace. We know at last the truth of what Chief Seattle wrote to President Pierce in 1854, that "to harm the earth is to heap abuse on its Creator."

If we know that the question of justice can no longer be finessed by the pretension of solving all problems through growth, that too is grace. And if we come to the sober realization that the exercise of American power in the world is not and has never been as beneficent as our leaders still say, that is grace.

Perhaps most importantly, we are beginning to recognize that the American style of wasteful consumerism depends upon the oppression of the earth and the poor, that it offers a bogus model to the world and leaves us spiritually unfilled. That too is grace.

If we know the grace of God's judgment, we may know also the grace of the future that God seeks to give and the joy as well as the cost, of participating in its coming. The signs are all around: in the changing lifestyles of what surely must be millions now who are gradually discovering ways of "living more with less"; in the thousands of citizens' advocacy and action groups around the country whereby ordinary people are taking control of their lives back from giant corporations and impersonal bureaucracies; in the new ways of working and the small-scale economic initiatives which insist that work must be personally fulfilling while respecting the environment and enhancing the lives of those for whom the product or service is rendered; and in the revitalization of the peace movement, with what may be the fulfillment of President Eisenhower's prophecy that one day the people of the world would want peace so badly that their leaders would have to get out of the way and let them have it.

We know the direction we have to move and many steps that we can take: toward *sufficiency* in the enjoyment of material things, with communities and institutions that eliminate the extremes of misery and affluence; toward harmony with nature and conservation of energy and other resources, so that the sufficiency can have *sustainability*; and toward an ethic of *solidarity* that overcomes the pride of class and the indignities of racism and sexism and gets on with the job of constructing an international order whereby the sustainable sufficiency may apply to *all*.

We need positive images of this better future to invigorate our movement toward it. There is no better source of inspiration for envisioning it than the biblical story itself. Perhaps we have emphasized too much that the consummation of God's kingdom lies beyond the historical process. Look at the biblical pictures again. Clearly the kingdom breaks into history. And clearly our faithfulness can be instrumental to its breaking in:

And I will make for you a covenant on that day with the beasts of the field, the birds of the air, and the creeping things of the ground; and I will abolish the bow, the sword, and war from the land; and I will make you lie down in safety. And I will betroth you to me forever; and I will betroth you to me in righteousness and justice, in steadfast love, and in mercy. I will betroth you to me in faithfulness; and you shall know the Lord. (Hosea 2:18-20)

WHEN THE VISION BREAKS DOWN
Land and Militarization

People are increasingly aware of the enormous economic and human cost of the arms race, even if we should never have a war. Nuclear winter, the final insult to our beautiful planet, is accepted now as a real threat by many competent scientists. Underestimated and often overlooked, however, are the damaging environmental realities already with us caused by our over-inflated trust in weapons to provide security.

Did you know that as much uranium mining (with all the dangers to people and the environment and the related problems of handling, transport, processing and storage) is done to produce weapons as to supply the nuclear power industry? There is increasing concern about where to store radioactive waste. Few communities willingly accept it. But not many people realize that substantially more radioactive waste is created through our nuclear weapons programs than by nuclear power plants!

Often forgotten are the victims of nuclear weapons testing: the people whose health is affected, or who are permanently displaced from their land; the islands damaged, some obliterated; the spoiled lagoons; the dirtied atmosphere. What about the effects of military bases upon the communities where they are located: the way they usurp limited space and resources; the political, economic and social problems they create for people whose livelihood has always been centered on the land?

And what about war itself? Those who live at a distance from war may or may not concern themselves with body counts. It is the local people who must bear the death and pain of warfare. Along with that, they bear immediate and long-term effects of defoliants and other strong pollutants of war, gaping bomb craters in their once-level rice paddies, the destruction of centuries-old irrigation and community water supply systems, the loss of treasured wildlife. But doesn't it affect us all?

What about the effect of our militaristic attitudes upon budgets and the utilization of scarce resources? How insatiable are the voracious appetites of militarization, not simply for the superpowers, but also and especially for their economically-poor third world "partners"!

In 1982 the military expenditures of developed countries were seventeen times larger than aid they gave countries in need. Twenty-five countries which since 1981 have had to reschedule their debt (many of them in severe foreign debt crisis) spent a total of eleven billion dollars for arms in that period!

With these distorted budgets it is indeed difficult to deal effectively with the burgeoning global environmental agenda and related human problems: industrial poisons, water and air pollution, erosion, desertification, poverty, famine.

— *B. David Williams*

MARSHALL ISLANDS MON AMOUR

by Darlene Keju-Johnson

Yokwe kom! Greetings from the Marshall Islands. The Marshallese people have been governed by the United States of America for more than thirty years. Soon after the U.S.A. took our island from Japan in World War II, it signed the United Nations Trusteeship agreement for Micronesia. In this agreement, the U.S.A. promised to protect our health and to prevent the loss of our lands and resources. It is a promise that the U.S.A. never kept.

Before we knew it, our islands were exploding into the air. In all, the U.S.A. tested sixty-six atomic and hydrogen bombs at Bikini and Enewetok Atolls—bombs which continue to affect the people today. During the testing, six islands were completely blown off the face of the earth.

In 1946, the U.S. military commander came to Bikini and told the people that the nuclear testing was "for the good of mankind and to end all world wars." The chief didn't really understand this, but one word stuck in his mind and that word was "mankind." He thought mankind was like God, so he told the military commander: "If the testing if for the good of God, then I will let my people go."

What the Americans didn't do was tell the people they would never see their islands again. Instead, the Americans promised the Bikinians that they could return home when the tests were finished. The Bikinians thought this would be very soon—perhaps a few weeks, or at most several months. What they didn't know was that they would never return to their home again.

The Bikinians were resettled three times and the Enewetok people, whose islands were used for 43 nuclear tests, also were relocated. They suffered many problems because the new islands did not have enough resources to support their growing populations. You can imagine the psychological problems the people had because of moving from one island to the next, without any explanations.

The sixty-six nuclear bomb tests contaminated hundreds of Marshallese and American servicemen with radioactive fallout during the 1950's. The list of health problems resulting from this exposure is virtually endless, and includes many cases of thyroid cancer, leukemia, cataracts, miscarriages and stillbirths. I have interviewed many women from the affected islands who have had more than four miscarriages.

Darlene Keju-Johnson is the first Marshallese to receive a Master's degree in Public Health. This article is taken from her presentation at the Sixth Assembly of the World Council of Churches, Vancouver, Canada, 1983, and is reprinted with permission.

The Marshallese describe these babies as "jelly fish." The baby is born on the labor table, and it breathes and moves up and down, but it is not shaped like a human being. It looks like a bag of jelly. These babies only live for a few hours. Sometimes, babies are born with growths like horns on their heads, while others have six fingers or toes.

I grew up on the Northern islands, which are downwind of Bikini and Enewetok. Today, I have three tumors in my body—one was taken out recently. I don't know what causes them, but like many Marshallese I am afraid for the future and I am concerned about what will happen if I have children.

Compounding this problem is the inadequate medical treatment provided by the U.S. Government. Instead of helping treat these radiation-related health problems, the U.S. Department of Energy (DOE) scientists use the people like "guinea pigs" in a scientific experiment. One statement, made by the U.S. scientists before allowing a group of Marshallese to return back to a radioactive island, demonstrated the lack of concern for the Marshallese: "Even though the radioactive contamination of Rongelap Island is considered perfectly safe for human habitation, the levels of activity are higher than those found in other inhabited locations in the world. The habitation of these people on the islands will afford most valuable radiation data on human beings."

Moreover, in thirty years, the U.S. DOE scientists have never provided the Marshallese with personal medical records or tried to explain their health problems to them. This is why the Marshallese are today requesting the help and support of doctors internationally who are independent of the U.S. Government to provide the necessary health care treatment and monitoring programs that the Marshallese so urgently need.

As if nuclear tests were not enough, the U.S.A. set up the Kwajalein Missile Range in the Marshalls to test its long-range nuclear missiles. These missiles are fired from Vandenberg Air Force Base in California and land in Kwajalein's once-peaceful lagoon. Again, the U.S.A. relocated hundreds of Marshallese from their home islands in Kwajalein for the missile testing. These people were moved to Ebeye Island, where today 8,000 people live crowded on this tiny sixty-six acre island.

The island has been called a "biological time bomb" and the hospital is so understaffed and so poor it cannot possibly provide adequate health care for the Marshallese. My family has lived on Ebeye for many years, and it was as I grew up that I experienced the U.S. military's racist discrimination against the Marshallese — an attitude that continues today.

Kwajalein Island, where the Americans live, with a first-class hospital, good schools, and numerous recreational facilities, is just three miles away. But it might as well be 3,000 miles away, for the Marshallese must obtain a pass before they can travel to their own islands. It is very difficult to gain access to Kwajalein's hospital, even in emergencies, and there have been many cases of children being refused entry into Kwajalein because they don't have a pass and then they die on their return to Ebeye.

It is the overcrowded conditions on Ebeye, combined with the fact that the people cannot use two-thirds of the lagoon for fishing or the islands for farming which makes the Kwajalein landowners feel like prisoners on Ebeye.

After thirty years of accepting this treatment as second-class citizens, the Kwajalein landowners got together in 1982 and sailed out to their off-limits island in Kwajalein Atoll. For four months, the people took back their islands in protest of the conditions on Ebeye and the discrimination on Kwajalein. More than 1,000 people set up camps on eleven islands. The people were glad to be on their own islands and felt a sense of freedom and peace. For many younger people it was the first time on these islands, and it felt good to eat food from the islands and do things that the people cannot do in Ebeye.

The protest, called "Operation Homecoming," forced the U.S.A. to make certain concessions to the Kwajalein landowners to help the problems on Ebeye. But the basic system of injustice remains today. Since signing a three-year lease for use of Kwajalein, the military's treatment of the Kwajalein people has gotten worse, with many new restrictions imposed on the Ebeye community.

All of this activity in the Marshall Islands has been to develop the most destructive weapons of war. Just this June, the U.S.A. tested the first MX missile at Kwajalein, and plans to continue with many more, including the Minuteman and Trident. The U.S.A. tells us that they are in our islands to protect us. But our response is: "Protect us from whom?" We do not have any enemies. You may be interested to know that there is no word in the Marshallese language for "enemy."

The Marshallese are known throughout Micronesia to be the most friendly people. We always invite people into our homes and give them food and whatever else we have to offer. But the U.S.A. has taken advantage of our kindness.

It is time we, the Marshallese people, controlled our islands. There is growing resentment against military presence at Kwajalein and it is only a matter of time before we remove the base. But we need your support. Without the help of people around the world, we will not be successful in bringing independent medical aid to our islands, or succeed in our struggle to determine our future.

The Heritage of Atomic Tests

In the 37 years since the atomic bomb was first "dropped" on the Marshalls at Bikini, the lives not only of the exiles from their homeland (Bikini and Enewetok), or the groups directly irradiated, but the lives of *all* Marshallese have been radically altered. The effects of radiation pervade their existence far beyond the readily observable and reported health and environmental effects associated with the extensive U.S. nuclear weapons testing program in the Marshalls. Today, in the broad sense, "radiation" is a basic, pervading reality for all Marshallese people.

Indeed, a new culture, vocabulary and mythology have developed around the radiation question. Whenever there is a physical debility, a birth anomaly or other abnormality, the people tend to believe that such had not occurred before "The Bomb." Cases of fish poisoning, unusual plant disease, the demise of the highly valued arrowroot plant (traditional staple), seem invariably to be attributed to radiation, even though this is contrary to scientific evidence. Myth or reality, these anxieties and fears are painfully real, and they are a consequence of the testing program.

The atoll groups most directly affected by ionizing radiation, each of which has had a particular claim before the United States Government through legal channels, need to be understood before there can be any clarity regarding the divisions, as well as the needs, of the people, and the current effects of radiation on their lives:

a) The Bikini people (now living on Kili, 500 miles southeast of the Bikini atoll) seemed adamant and single-minded that their island must be cleaned up and made inhabitable by the United States Government. They are culturally, emotionally, and historically tied to their land: an incomplete, unhappy people removed from it. They were evacuated thirty-seven years ago and now compare themselves to "something floating on the water, looking for a place to land," or "the children of Israel, waiting to go to the Promised Land." They feel betrayed by the U.S. Government and insist that the U.S.A. must, however belatedly, keep its initial promise to return them to their island "in a short while." As evidenced by the U.S. attempts at decontaminating Enewetok, the cleanup of Bikini would be very costly and limited in its effectiveness. Bikinians, however, cannot believe that the U.S.A. is unable to clean up Bikini. "The U.S.A. landed on the moon. The U.S.A. can destroy the world in thirty minutes," they argue. "Why can't they clean up Bikini?" But they were told by an American official: "No... can you peel the water out of the Atlantic?"

b) The people from the Enewetok atoll perceive that the scientists are giving them incorrect and conflicting messages. They have been told that they can return to their island (as many of them have), yet as they look at what is happening to their people, they fear that the island is really not safe. They live with the reality of what they call "the tomb," where the wastes cleaned up from Enewetok Island have been buried in a huge cement-domed pit on the island of Runit — a part of the Enewetok atoll. There are also three other islands which have been completely destroyed and are no longer even visible. Obviously, the island of Runit is not usable. The Enewetok people insist on heavy reparations payments from the U.S.A., with the possibility of themselves controlling and investing that money. They feel that their way of life has been wrested from them and will accept money in large amounts as inadequate, though the only possible compensation for what they have suffered.

c) The Rongelap people, fallout victims of a 1954 blast, are deeply troubled by an inadequate supply of edible (uncontaminated) local food. They are now living on their island, but several of the islands in the atoll have been declared "off limits" by the U.S. Department of Energy (DOE), and they fear that their children will be affected from eating contaminated foods. Birth defects have become a source of deep anxiety and we found the people to be discouraged and cynical about their future.

Excerpted from "Marshall Islands: 37 Years After," Report of a World Council of Churches Delegation to the Marshall Islands, 1983. Published by the W.C.C. Commission of the Churches on International Affairs, 1983.

CHANGING OUR LIFESTYLES
Changing our World

by Earl Arnold

Most people resist the idea of an eco-just lifestyle because they perceive it as "bad news." They cling to the false expectation that there is unlimited material progress ahead—as they unconscionably tolerate the poverty of others.

We offer the eco-just lifestyle as good news—more joyous, more fun, more healthy and fulfilling because it is more authentically human, more in tune with the way we human creatures were supposed to behave on this lovely, bounteous, vulnerable planet.

Eco-justice requires a change of heart to live out. It goes way beyond self-interest. And unless the lifestyle changes we make are deeply rooted in faith, they will not be easy. But if our eco-just lifestyle is a spiritual move,

and we are open to the love that undergirds us, it can become our joy as well as our task.

— Bill Gibson

"Lifestyle" involves an outlook, a state of mind, a way of understanding the world and ourselves. It is mirrored in the material trappings with which we surround ourselves. Our lifestyle encompasses our work and our play, the things we choose to eat and the place we choose to sleep. It includes the things we spend our money on and what we do with the money we don't spend: our savings, investment and giving patterns. Our lifestyle is particularly evidenced in our relationships with others: the people we live with and work with, our neighbors near and distant, with whom we share in face-to-face contact or through the channels of business and government.

Each of us has a lifestyle, and with the wide variety of lifestyles in vogue in America we have all exercised a certain amount of choice in it. What kind of lifestyle,

---

Earl Arnold is Associate Coordinator, Eco-Justice, of the Center for Religion, Ethics and Social Policy, Ithaca, NY.

though, have we chosen? What makes a choice of lifestyle a "responsible" choice? What difference does our lifestyle choice make in today's world?

In their resource book for camping programs, *Lifestyles of Faithfulness* (see Bibliography), Charles and Carol McCollough characterize the dominant American lifestyle patterns as "lifestyles of conquest and defeat." People who live these lifestyles view life, consciously or unconsciously, as a contest. The strong, the determined, the resourceful win, and the others lose. Our national mythology fosters just this understanding of life: the American hero struggles against formidable odds, wrestling wealth from untamed field and forest, and defending any gain against aborigines and encroaching neighbors. It takes no great wit to apply this same philosophy to the day-to-day adventure of living.

A "lifestyle of conquest and defeat" pits each person against every other, interfering with the ability of the human community to work together for the common good. Instead of cooperation, patterns of domination and oppression flourish and injustice runs unchecked. Since the earth is treated as an adversary rather than a partner in survival, there is no sense of stewardship, of responsibility to respect nature and preserve its productive capacity for the future.

But conquest is only one side of the "lifestyle of conquest and defeat." Not everyone can be a winner. Thousands of Americans feel defeated, embittered, and without self-esteem or a stake in the social order. Thus the underside of the dominant American lifestyle causes great loss to individuals as well as to the social enterprise.

In contrast to the "lifestyle of conquest and defeat," we would like to propose what the McColloughs call "lifestyles of faithfulness." They connect these lifestyles with the concept of *shalom,* the Hebrew word for "peace": "We seek this *shalom* in nature by our gentle use of it. We seek this *shalom* in people by expecting God's presence in them. These two aspects of our lifestyles constitute faithfulness to God, *shalom,* and abundant lives."

A BETTER ALTERNATIVE

Is lifestyle change worthwhile? Does it have a place in an effective strategy for making the world a better place for all? Thoughtful people sometimes raise objections: that lifestyle is a middle-class concern, that the impact of lifestyle changes is trivial, and that it distracts from the serious business of changing political, economic and social structures.

First, let us admit that lifestyle change does begin with individuals, and it begins with modest, even rather trivial, changes in their way of life. To make the world better, it must be part of a long-term strategy, looking for changes over years and decades. But lifestyle change is something an individual *can* do (though we recommend a group process to provide encouragement and support for the individual's effort). And we suggest it as a starting point for persons who want to work for a just and sustainable world. The program of lifestyle change we propose includes an element of advocacy, for individuals to begin to speak out in their communities and to write to their representatives in government in support of structural changes that will make our world more eco-just.

In a certain sense, lifestyle *is* a middle-class issue, addressed primarily to a middle-class audience. The lifestyle changes we suggest, in the direction of greater simplicity, more community, with less consumption of material goods, make sense in light of the highly consumptive lifestyle of most middle-class Americans. For the majority of people in the world, an eco-just lifestyle would involve consuming *more* food, *more* energy, having a greater degree of financial security and control over their destiny! But, by and large, it is middle-class interests that prevent the establishment of a more just and more ecologically balanced world order. The current systems of domination and exploitation are kept in place by the demands of middle-class Americans and others, who demand that enough of the spoils of the "lifestyle of conquest and defeat" be available to keep the contest interesting and maintain their accustomed comforts.

One goal of lifestyle change is to provide an example of a satisfying lifestyle that does not have to be maintained through a military-industrial complex that destroys the earth and oppresses people around the globe. As eco-just lifestyles are seen and understood by middle-class people in the United States and in other industrialized countries, it will be easier for people who benefit from the current system to realize that the alternative to conquest is not necessarily defeat.

The true power of lifestyle change cannot be appreciated unless it is seen as involving more than the material trappings of the way we live. Our lifestyle is tied up with the way we look at the world, with the intellectual, emotional and spiritual roots of our lives. The way I read the newspaper is changed; the way I vote; the way I talk with friends and neighbors about community and world issues.

If we measure the value of lifestyle change by the number of watts saved or grams of protein not consumed or tons of aluminum recycled, it may not amount to much. But if we look for its value in transformed minds, in changed outlooks, in reinvigorated communities, its significance could be very large, and it could make a real contribution toward changing our world. It is in this arena that I see the real contribution of lifestyle issues toward the achievement of a just and sustainable world.

STEWARDSHIP AND ECONOMICS

by William E. Gibson

Christians properly understand the care of the earth as the care of God's creation: a human task succinctly summed up in Genesis 2:15 when the Lord God puts the human creature in the garden "to till it and keep it." We are to till it for our own sustenance; and we are to keep it, not only because coming generations will require it for their sustenance, but because its Creator and Owner regards it as very good and therefore to be cherished, not just for our sake but for God's.

This, of course, is what we mean by the stewardship of the earth, a responsibility now receiving renewed emphasis precisely because humankind has so badly botched it up. The past two centuries are notable for the heedless use of science and technology to conquer nature without really caring for it. The human activity supposedly served by this attempted conquest is economics.

Ironically, the subordination of stewardship to economics violates the fundamental meaning and purpose of the economy itself. The very words "stewardship" and "economy" are English translations of the same Greek word, *oikonomia*. The steward is a servant responsible for planning and conducting the affairs of a household. Blessed, said Jesus, is "the faithful and wise steward [whose master has] set over his household, to give them their portion of food at the proper time." (Luke 12:42) He is blessed, that is, when his master comes and finds him so doing (Luke 12:43).

Stewardship is the faithful and wise management of a household. We extend the meaning to encompass all that is involved in tilling and keeping the garden, the faithful and wise use of God's creation. But economics, like stewardship, means the management of a household, and the meaning extends beyond a single household to the whole society. Economics means the arrangements in a society for producing and distributing the goods and services that the members of the society, that is, the larger household, require for their sustenance and fulfillment. And so economics and stewardship are identical when those arrangements, which depend absolutely on the good things of God's creation, are both faithful and wise.

NEITHER UNEMPLOYMENT NOR POVERTY

The proper purpose of economics is not the maximization of production or of profit, because that would be bad stewardship, destructive of the earth's continuing fruitfulness. The purpose is provision of sufficient and sustainable sustenance for all. Stewardship in economics means making arrangements, constructing and maintaining a system, under which each person according to his or her gifts of talent and ability participates in the work of meeting the needs and enriching the life of the household. Each member contributes to the common enterprise; each has or receives enough for health and fulfillment. Stewardship in economics carries out the present and future intention of the Creator that all be filled with good things. (Ps. 104:28 *et passim*) Therefore it tolerates neither unemployment nor poverty.

To respond faithfully to the problem of unemployment we have to begin by viewing economic life and human work as squaring with God's will only to the extent that they are expressions of stewardship, the faithful and wise management of the household. In the well-managed household you do not see some members growing fat while others starve. You do not see limited provisions required for the long term used up before the proper time. You do not find dangerous wastes that make the house unsafe to live in. You do not see some members exhausting themselves in hard labor while others goof off. And if labor-saving devices reduce the amount of labor necessary, everybody enjoys some additional leisure and play or else engages in new kinds of good work to enhance further the common life of the household. Some may get special rewards for taking on certain tasks that are particularly difficult, onerous, or dangerous or particularly creative, original, or beneficial. Limited departures from equality in enjoyment of goods produced, however, are justified only as in some way they serve to improve conditions for others in the household, particularly those who are most vulnerable or in need of special protection and care, such as the children, the aged, and the handicapped. Nobody's luxuries can take precedence over anybody's necessities. The household is organized more for

---

William E. Gibson is coordinator, Eco-Justice Project and Network, Center for Religion, Ethics and Social Policy, Ithaca, New York.

cooperation than for competition, with the aim of making sure that the most important work gets done, while making the most of each person's special gifts, so that his or her work may be at once both as enjoyable and as useful as possible.

Now this, of course, is an idealized picture of the way a household works, although it is recognizable, I believe, as indicative of the way a good family functions. And if it is not recognizable as a picture of American capitalism, it still is relevant as a standard by which to ascertain how far our political economy has departed from discharging its proper functions. For there can be no faithful stewardship of creation unless stewardship in the sense of long-term sustainability and wholeness is understood as an essential function and criterion of economic life. Neither can there be any solution to the problem of unemployment, or substantial elimination of the destitution and misery coexisting with affluence and wastefulness in this land of plenty, unless justice in the sense of an equitable sufficiency for all, without extravagance and wastefulness by anyone, is understood as another necessary function and criterion of economic life. And these functions and criteria — sustainability and sufficiency — are rooted in the most fundamental, normative imperative of biblical faith, the *love* that is the one summary word for the activity and the will of God, the love that affirms the solidarity of all members of the household or the society, insisting that sufficiency must be for all and that it must be sustainable for the sake of the whole creation and the generations yet to come.

TEN THINGS WE NEED
To Take Part in an Eco-just Future

1. VISION
A vision of the kind of world we want to have, a world in which people have all they need—not just in terms of material necessities, but also in terms of having work to do and the essentials for health, creativity and spiritual growth. This vision is of a world where the human family exists in a harmonious relationship with nature.

2. SHOCK
A sense of crisis, of utmost urgency, because what we are talking about is life versus death. We need to grasp the great new fact of our time: that there are ecological limits. They show up in issues of energy shortages, toxic wastes, hunger, the rich-poor gap, nuclear weapons controversies, inflation and economic stagnation. The very survival of life is at stake.

3. EDUCATION
Schools need to change their agendas if students are to know what is going on and be equipped to live responsibly in today's world. Alternative and informal education can go a long way to counteract present educational deficiencies and help people of all ages understand the crisis.

4. LEADERSHIP
We need leaders in politics, education, religion, labor and citizens' organizations who can articulate people's concerns and aspirations. They must be able to move out ahead and bring their constituencies to heightened consciousness and new purpose.

5. SACRIFICE
For the sake of the health and wholeness of people and nature, some people must be willing to speak unpopular truths, risk political defeat, side with the poor, risk poverty themselves, buck the establishment, extend themselves in volunteer work — i.e., "find life by losing it."

6. SECURITY
People need protection from the insecurities of unemployment, illness, the cost of education, retirement and old age. When burdens become too acute, people may lose their moral sensitivity and fight viciously for their own survival. The solution lies not only in public measures of security, but in nurturing families and communities in which people bear one another's burdens.

7. EQUALITY IN SHARING THE COSTS OF CHANGE
Polls indicate that most people see the need for appropriate lifestyle changes. But the ordinary citizen is not encouraged to practice simplicity and frugality when tax legislation favors the rich. Industries pollute because it is expensive not to; disarmament threatens defense workers; powerful special interests in govern-

ment cause legislation and policy-making to be unfair. If the cost of change were equally borne, a sense of common purpose might emerge and change might happen much more quickly.

8. PERCEPTION OF NEXT STEPS

These are huge changes we're talking about. People need specific, simple steps to move in the right direction right away. Changes can be made in patterns of consuming, conserving, working, sharing, playing, eating, advocating and giving.

9. HOPE

People are paralyzed unless they have hope: hope that a good future is possible, that nuclear holocaust is preventable, that pollution can be cleaned up, that hunger and poverty can be overcome, that the earth's population can be kept within its carrying capacity. Hope comes when visions become clear, leaders prove trustworthy, communities become supportive, next steps make sense, progress becomes observable and religious faith is deepened.

10. FAITH

...that life is to be celebrated, that the One behind the phenomena of this world is a friend and not an enemy and that ultimately, all will be well. Faith helps us act without seeing fruits. Faith also includes love which wills the good of the neighbor—and that includes not only the whole family, but generations not yet born and the whole non-human creation, too.

"GOD'S VOICE IS THE VOICE OF ALL NATURE..."

by Cecil Corbett

The earth is the Lord's and the fulness thereof, the world and those who dwell therein. (Psalm 24:1)

Chief Joseph of the Nez Perce tribe declared, "The earth and myself are of one mind, recognizing the sacredness of all things, every rock, animal and plant. We are all made from the same elements. We are all manifestations of the mystery." As a member of the Nez Perce tribe, I, too, was taught from early childhood the sacredness of all things. I was taught that from the common source, from the mystery, come *Homo sapiens*, the fish of the sea, the plants and animals of desert and forest and the birds of the air. And to that common source we shall return.

The concept of respect for creation is common to all Indian tribes. Indians have tried to live in harmony with creation and not to exploit it for individual profit. Very few tribes have any concept of individual ownership of land. They believe, rather, that to have land simply means to be steward of that part of God's creation.

As Chief Black Hawk of the Sauk tribe of the Great Lakes area described it: "My reason teaches me that the land cannot be sold. The Great Spirit gave it to His children to live upon and cultivate as far as it is necessary for their subsistence. They have a right to the soil. Nothing can be sold but such things as can be carried away."

This theme is repeated again and again. From a Blackfoot Indian: "We cannot sell the lives of men and animals. Therefore we cannot sell this land. It was put here for us by the Great Spirit and we cannot sell it because it does not belong to us."

In many Indian tribes, an initiation ritual called the youth's vigil enabled boys to experience first hand the supportive and challenging forces of nature. The vigil took place at the time of puberty; a youth would go into the forest alone to fast for many days. It was a test of fortitude, a time to learn appreciation for all the land provided, and also a time to gain the insight that each person has a responsibility towards all Creation.

The concept of land as "mother" is common in the prose and poetry of the Navajo. Each Navajo feels a great debt to Mother Earth, and respect for her gifts penetrates the very fiber of his or her way of life. A brief study of the history of the Navajos, as well as that of

Dr. Cecil Corbett, a member of the Nez Perce tribe of Idaho, is president of Cook Christian Training School in Tempe, AZ. He is a minister of The Presbyterian Church (U.S.A.).

other tribes, will reveal that they survived for centuries by observing and respecting nature's cycles. During a time of drought, a community would scatter to take advantage of the few remaining plants and animals. During a time of plenty, they would gather once again in community to plan for the winter and times of scarcity.

NATIVE AMERICAN THEOLOGICAL REFLECTION

Native Americans live so close to the land that they know both its abundance and its limitations. They know that seasons of plenty are often followed by seasons of want. They know that the land and its gifts have to be treated with respect and nurtured for future use. Above all, in order to maintain harmony, they consciously revere the Great Spirit who rules over the world. All this has influenced their life and prayers.

There is kinship between the Indian and the Old Testament Psalmist when they express appreciation for God's creative power and the beauty of the earth. So often, we forget that the Psalms are not mere poems but are actually prayers of adoration and supplication. At Cook Christian Training School in Tempe, Arizona, Indian students cast English translations of the Psalms into Indian thought-patterns. This has proved to be a thought-provoking, challenging experience.

Psalm 19 was translated thus by a student named Hospevela:

The power of the Great Spirit above has been shown by the making of the stars of the heavens, and the brightness of the lights in the sky is wonderful.

God's voice is the voice of all nature, and God's wisdom shows even in the darkness of the night. The whole earth is filled with the melody of God.

In the days of creation God sent forth the great sun shining like the brightness of the face of a lover, and God's strength warms all the world.

The law of the Great Spirit can do all good things and God's words bring wisdom to simple souls.

Follow the way laid out by the Great Spirit of wisdom and it will bring you in peace and contentment to a fine reward.

Wash my heart, oh God, that the wicked things of earth gain not a victory over me, for I would stand straight like an arrow, looking up and not bending down with any wrongdoing.

May my lips speak aright—may my heart think aright, oh, thou who are the strength of my life and the savior of my soul.

Is there a Native American theology? One might respond that there is no *one* such theology. Rather, there are many tribal expressions of one idea: respect for the Creator and Creation. This continues to be the central theme of the Native American's world view and ethos. It is more than appreciation for the beauty of Creation. It is recognition of the necessary interrelatedness between all living creatures.

Chief Luther Standing Bear of the Sioux wrote about what happens when people have contempt for Creation. "The old Lakota was wise," he wrote. "He knew that man's heart away from nature became hard; he knew that lack of respect for growing, living things soon led to lack of respect for humans, too. So he kept his youth close to its softening influence."

THE KINSHIP OF ALL CREATION

The choice is clearly before us: Should we use up our limited resources and let future generations fend for themselves? Or do we live a life of stewardship and respect for God's creation.

American Indians in 1984 hold title to 55 million acres of land. Much of it is virgin land that holds promise for energy needs. Uranium, coal and geothermal resources are now found on Native American reservations and there is great concern that such wealth will be greedily exploited. And what about industries that continue to contaminate and deplete nonrenewable resources? Or acid rain that continues to harm the atmosphere? Or radiation on Navajo reservations that continues to reach fearful levels due to ground water seepage?

The story is told that when the Navajo people heard that the atom bomb had been dropped on Hiroshima and Nagasaki, medicine men offered prayers of penitence. They suspected that the uranium for the bomb had been mined on their reservations and they viewed this as the ultimate defiance of human responsibility for dominion over the earth. We were created to subdue the earth and to enjoy it, but not to use it to subdue and to kill other human beings.

"How we delude ourselves. . .When we consider the immensity of the universe, we must confess that man is insignificant." wrote Albert Schweitzer. "Man's life can hardly be considered the goal of the universe. Its margin of existence is always so precarious. Man is ethical only when he considers every living cell, whether plant or animal, sacred and divine."

Chief Luther Standing Bear knew from his experience that the person who sat on the ground in a tipi meditating on life and its meaning, accepting the kinship of all creatures and acknowledging unity with the universe of things was infusing into his or her being the true essence of civilization. When men and women ignore this, their humanizing abilities will cease.

LEADERS' GUIDES

*You give breath, fresh life begins,
  you keep renewing the world.
    (Psalm 104:30, The Jerusalem Bible)*

"CARING FOR GOD'S EARTH"
A Guide for Leaders
by Carolyn Hardin Engelhardt

Welcome to an experience in which you will discover yourself to be a capable, influential person, interrelated and interdependent with all that God has created. We are meant to be stewards under God, not dominators of the landscape. We are meant to be neighbors to all created things. Of course, discovering the way to this relationship is not easy; many powerful forces from outside and from within ourselves keep us from approaching it. But when we learn about God's earth in an active way—that is, when we are making decisions, using our imaginations, listening to other people and speaking out of our own experience, we can learn to see ourselves as stewards and neighbors. That is the purpose of this study guide.

The five sessions that follow may be used with adults or with youth. The most enriching possibility would be to explore them with people of different generations, backgrounds and expectations.

As a leader, you may find within these pages methods and ideas that are new to you. Be grateful! That means that you, too, can learn alongside those you have agreed to "guide." You need not be an expert on every subject when you are the leader. Rather, you are the one who sets the stage for exploration and discovery.

Caring for God's earth is not just an option for "environmentalists" or highly-motivated groups of people. It is the outcome of *being* God's people. It means we understand those three words—*caring, God's* and *earth*—with our hearts and minds. It means we grasp the concept of the whole earth's interdependence.

OBJECTIVES

Consider some of the following possible objectives of the study you are about to lead:
1. To enable ordinary Christians to see themselves as influential, empowered and courageous individuals when they face issues related to the water and land they depend on.
2. To enable people to see alternative lifestyles as real possibilities, and to help them find many more options for action than they ever thought they had.
3. To enable people to see water and land as their concern simply because they, too, are created and interrelated with all of Creation.
4. To help people see what caring for God's earth has to do with being stewards and neighbors.

As you prepare for these study sessions, consider finding a leadership team that includes both youth and adults. Or using a different team for each session. The sessions will certainly be stronger if you have team leadership; there will be more heads and hands to share in the preparation and to lend support when you are trying out new approaches. Teams of leaders can also spread the word about the study by their own informal networks of friends and colleagues.

PUBLICITY

Publicity before, during and after the study is as essential as preparing for the study sessions themselves. Create anticipation. Give people a chance to note the dates on their calendars long in advance. Let people know what they can expect to learn from the study. With good pre-publicity, people who plan to participate will begin to notice environmental issues all around them—in the news, in the attitudes and actions of others and in their own behavior.

Keep publicity going during the study as well. Those who missed a session can stay up-to-date through newsletter reports on what took place in the last session. Even people who do not participate can feel ownership of "what our church is doing." Put up displays, posters, charts, news and announcements about the group's study each week. Help everyone in the church feel part of it.

After the study, keep the subject alive! Caring for God's earth is not something we finish. Perhaps your church

---

Carolyn Hardin Engelhardt is a church program ministries consultant, trainer, educator and writer. She lives in Cheshire, CT.

will decide to make changes. Perhaps your study group will implement certain decisions. Follow the progress of everyone who is struggling to care for God's earth.

HOW TO USE THIS STUDY

1. PRO-EARTH's collection of readings is intended as background preparation for leaders and participants. It is assumed that leaders will read the entire book before the study begins. Participants can be given selections from the book to read at their own pace, which is how most people will read it anyway. A particular session may motivate participants to go home and read other sections of the book. As the study progresses, people may find related newspaper or magazine articles; encourage them to bring these to the meetings and share them with the group. PRO-EARTH is not the only resource; let the readings expand.

2. Use this guide as the basis for five or more sessions during Lent, during a missional emphasis, for church school or for a youth fellowship series.

3. Use "Caring for God's Earth" as the theme for a retreat. You might divide the sessions into Friday night, Saturday morning, Saturday afternoon, Saturday night, and Sunday morning.

4. For a week-long camp or vacation church school, you might use each session plan for a different day and build the whole day's experiences around the themes.

5. Each of the session plans incorporates these five emphases:

- biblical images that compel, impel and sustain us:
- imagining the future;
- identifying lifestyle choices;
- identifying possible stewardship actions by individuals, small groups or institutions;
- increasing global awareness.

Suggest that the group build a festival around the theme "Caring for God's Earth." Plan for five rooms of activities—one room for each of the above emphases. Give out tickets so that people can visit each room in somewhat equal numbers for a specific period of time. Plan it so that the festival lasts all day and includes a meal. Use the mealtime to illustrate the theme. Invite the whole community!

Such a festival might be organized by those who have already participated in the study. Leaders in each room can explain each emphasis. Activities can be drawn from those in the session plans. On the other hand, a "Caring for God's Earth" festival might be the way participants approach the study theme to begin with, rather than letting the festival be the outgrowth of the study series. Which is the best way for your community?

SESSION ONE: INTRODUCTION TO THE THEME "CARING FOR GOD'S EARTH"

PREPARATION

1. Place a large map of the world and some large sheets of paper on the wall.

2. Have ready: paper and pencils; magazines with pictures than can represent food, self-sufficiency and interdependence; scissors and glue; large paper for collage; paints, brushes or other painting implements; Connections Game Board; markers and chart paper.

EXPERIENCING GOD'S EARTH

1. As people enter the room, ask them to make a list of all the foods they have eaten that day. Next to each item, have them write down what state, province or country that food most likely came from. Now, on the map, note *where* these places are. Discuss these places and think what sort of prayer would be appropriate for the group to pray regarding each place, its people, its situation, its land and water. Discuss what members of this group would have to do to be part of the *action* the prayer requires. The group may want to write the prayer down to use in a worship service later on, or pray extemporaneously at this point.

2. As a group, make a collage or painting about self-sufficiency and interdependence as it relates to people having enough food across the world.

3. Look at the words on the Connections Game Board. Tell the group that they don't have to be "experts" about these concepts, that whatever they already know is enough to start understanding what being a steward and a neighbor on God's earth is about. Ask each participant to choose one word from the game board and to tell the entire group *one* thing they know about that word or concept: "My word is _____. What I know about it is that _____."

4. Divide into small groups, each one having one of the following quotes to think about. Each group should finish these three statements concerning their quote: "By the year 2000, _____ will be *possible*." "By the year 2000, _____ will be *probable*." By the year 2000, _____ will be *preferable*." The groups may complete more than one of each of these statements if they wish.

Here are the quotes:

1) "If present trends continue, the world in 2000 will be more crowded, more polluted, less stable ecologically, and more vulnerable to disruption than the one we live in now." ("The Search for a New Humility," page 67)

2) "...the U.S. [should] make the elimination of hunger the primary focus of its relations with developing countries." ("The Search for a New Humility," page 67).

3) "We live in a world in which pollution is caused by the improper disposal of chemicals like benzene, toluene, trichlorophenol, hexachlorocyclohexane and octachlorocyclopentene." ("The Search for a New Bowl and Salt," page 59)

4) "...church-related agencies may be the *only* institutions in the country possessing the power and tenacity to resolve a number of the important problems about toxic and hazardous wastes." ("Love Canal Update," page 60)

5) "The U.S.A. tells us that they are in our islands to protect us. But our response is: 'Protect us from whom?' We do not have any enemies...there is no word in the Marshallese language for 'enemy'." ("Marshall Islands Mon Amour," page 73)

6) "'We're left to see if it is possible for us to embrace solidarity with the dispossessed...' This...is the challenge before us as the church in the midst of the current crisis in the American countryside." ("A Letter to the Churches," page 35)

7) "The forecast for the immediate and distant future is bleak. The present and potential destruction caused by acid rain is staggering, both economically and aesthetically." ("Creation Suffers," page 47)

8) "The American consumer is not alone in being endangered [by pesticides]. Widespread illiteracy, ignorance and poor working conditions in developing countries also take their toll." ("Pesticides—A Global Affair," page 41)

9) "We offer the eco-just lifestyle as *good news*. More joyous, more fun, more healthy and fulfilling because...it is more in tune with the way we human creatures were supposed to behave on this lovely, bounteous, vulnerable planet." ("Changing Our Lifestyle, Changing Our World," page 75)

10) "...recognition of the necessary interrelatedness between all living creatures." ("God's Voice is the Voice of All Nature," page 81)

11) "Changes can be made in patterns of consuming, conserving, working, sharing, playing, eating, advocating and giving." ("Ten Things We Need," page 79)

Ask all the groups to share their statements with the whole group. Identify the ones which reflect an attitude of stewardship and neighborliness.

5. Read Psalm 24:1 from *The Jerusalem Bible*: "To Yahweh belong earth and all it holds, the world and all who live in it." Identify those times when we are tempted to behave as though this is not true. Have someone read the verse again and as a group, pray for our growth in living out the vision of the Psalmist.

MORE WAYS TO EXPLORE "CARING FOR GOD'S EARTH"

1. Read the article "After the Uranium Spill" and as a group, make a timeline of what occurred in that story. After making the timeline, divide into three small groups. Have one group mark in blue what individuals did; another mark in red what small groups did, and the third group mark in green what institutions did. Then share your findings.

2. As a group, list any ways you can think of that God's earth has been cared for over the last ten years. Identify with blue those efforts made by individuals, with red those efforts made by small groups, and with green those efforts made by institutions.

3. The following is a list of situations that may continue to exist in the year 2000. For each of these situations, identify first what needs to happen for these conditions to continue until 2000. Second, identify what needs to be happening for these conditions *not* to exist in the year 2000. You may want to identify the distinct roles of individuals, small groups and institutions in each of these scenarios.

1) Industries are moving to developing countries where there are few regulations to protect the earth and people from pollution, hazardous waste, etc.

2) River basins are shared by two to ten countries and there is a growing demand for water.

3) Disposing of hazardous waste on land continues.

4) Outdoor club membership is growing.

5) Half the world's people are without reasonable access to a safe and adequate water supply.

6) In the last decade, Americans have cut their energy consumption significantly.

SESSION TWO: AIR

PREPARATION

1. Make the four signs for Activity 1. Gather feathers, a paper cup, ten feet of string, two chairs, an empty clear bottle, enough balloons for everyone, a Bible. Get ready a filmstrip projector, screen and cassette player and the filmstrip "A Void of Desolation?" You'll also need a long roll of paper, crayons, paper and pencils. For the last part of the section, you'll need the Connections Game Board and hymnals.

2. Read the biblical texts indicated.

3. Decide which leader will lead each experience and how much time you will spend on each.

EXPERIENCING AIR

1. As people arrive, have the following activities and signs ready in the four corners of the room to help them begin to think about air and biblical images related to air.

   A. Display a box with feathers at the bottom. The sign reads: *Blow these feathers and think: Do I have dominion over these feathers? Control over them? Can I be a partner with them?*

   B. Poke a small hole in the bottom of a paper cup and put a piece of string about 10 feet long through it. Then tie each end of the string to a chair and try to blow the cup from one end to the other. The sign reads *Blow the cup to the end of the string. Think about what you are doing. Is it more like being a servant, a ruler or a neighbor?*

   C. Have a Bible and a bottle with a lid ready. The sign reads: *Blow into this empty bottle and quickly put the lid on it. Read I Corinthians 12:12-26. Then look at this bottle of air—and think about it!*

   D. Put balloons on the table. The sign reads: *Blow up a balloon. Bounce it in the air and ask yourself repeatedly, "Am I your neighbor?"* It might be interesting to use a fan during this experience.

   People may freely go from one activity to the next as they gather.

2. In order for the group members to think more specifically about their *own* experiences of air, lead one of these activities:

   A. Ask people to watch for answers to some of the following questions as they watch the filmstrip, "A Void of Desolation?"
   - What is the main purpose of air?
   - What products do *you* have at home that cause air pollution when they are manufactured?
   - What activities do you engage in that cause air pollution—e.g., the use of fires, car travel, aerosols, microwaves, poor car maintenance, etc.?
   - List the dangers to the air that are shown in the film.

   B. On a long roll of paper divided in half lengthwise, ask people to write these captions along the bottom half: *If one part is hurt, all parts are hurt with it. If one part is given special honor, all parts enjoy it.* (I Cor. 12:26) On the top half of the paper, illustrate these concepts as they relate to air.

3. By now, people should be understanding more about how they live in relation to air. We are ready to bring the story of our faith together with our experience of air.

   Ask each participant to hold a blown balloon while you read the following passages from Scripture: I Cor. 12:12-26 and Luke 10:29-37.

   Ask: "How does the message of these scriptures compare to or differ from our experience with air?"

4. Ask group members to consider what these scriptures require of us by giving them of the following tasks:

   A. Discuss the following situations in small groups:
   - You have a car that can use either no-lead gas or leaded gas. Should you use no-lead gas in order to care for God's earth, even though it is more expensive?
   - Your church has been planning to install solar panels. Recently a building permit was granted for a high-rise office building on the south side of your church. It will bring in considerable tax income to the town. It will also prevent your use of solar panels.
   - A developer was willing to buy your land and develop it, except that the odors from your neighbor's dairy farm have recently made him waver.

   B. Write your pledge related to air.

5. Ask members of the group to bring in newspaper articles related to water and land. Put up a bulletin board where they can post their clippings. As the group does this they will grow in their awareness of the extent to which local, national and international issues are related to caring for God's earth. Their confidence in their own ability to think about these issues and make informed decisions will increase.

6. Hand out the Connections Game Board. Play Game 1: "Twenty Questions." This game will help people think ahead to all the topics to be explored in this study. The instructions are on page 91.

7. Sing together "For the Beauty of the Earth." Or repeat your group's pledge related to air, then sing the hymn and close with prayer.

MORE WAYS TO EXPLORE THE AIR AROUND US

1. Find and sing hymns about air, breath and breathing. Ask yourselves about the concepts in each hymn, such as: neighbor, steward, interdependence, a global perspective, all of Creation.

2. Ask different persons or small groups to produce time lines related to each of the following: What happens to hairspray after 10 minutes or an hour? a campfire? pollen? exhaust? pesticide sprays? sound waves? balloons let loose in a celebration? What is the human factor in these time lines? What do these time lines say about what people value? What part do groups or institutions have in what happens in these time lines?

3. Take a field trip to an appropriate site that will help the group to think about air. Some possibilities might include: a factory, an observatory, an experiment station or windmill. Prepare questions for which you would like to find answers so that participants will approach the field trip as alert and active learners.

4. Plan a research activity in which group members survey or observe their community to discover what good things are being done to protect the quality of air. Report back.

5. You may be able to borrow a parachute from a school or recreation agency. Ask all group members to stand around the edges of the parachute and gently lift it up and down. What happens when you work together? What happens when you do not work together? Can you move the parachute at different speeds? How does it feel when you stand underneath the parachute?

6. Using soap-bubble blowers may also increase your awareness of air. Can you control the air? Can you control what happens to the soap-bubbles?

7. Use kites to discover the air currents.

8. Make mobiles out of paper on which you have written important concepts about air. Display these in the church so that the whole congregation can consider them. You may wish to make other mobiles from recycled junk materials.

9. Read Psalm 96:11-13 to remember God's promises of justice and well-being for all Creation when there is *shalom*.

10. What biblical passage or image comes to your mind as you view frames 2-7, 12, 14, 20, or 23 in the filmstrip, "A Void of Desolation?" Does it relate to caretaker, dominion, steward or neighbor?

11. Find out where in your community there are examples of preservation being placed above profit.

SESSION THREE: WATER

PREPARATION

1. Prepare and display containers of clean water, dirty water and polluted water.

2. Post the news clippings the group has collected during the week.

3. Prepare Game 2, "Connections," and Game 6, "Steward-Neighbor."

4. Arrange to have copies of the article "Who Owns This Land?" for the group members, along with paper and pencils.

5. Practice the "Rainstorm" motions.

6. Gather enough bowls and jugs of water for each person, and perhaps a couple of towels.

7. Decide who will lead which experience.

8. Set up chairs and tables appropriately.

9. Think of ways a prayer might conclude the meditation.

EXPERIENCING WATER

1. Display in a prominent place three containers of water to get people started thinking about clean water, dirty water and polluted water.

2. Ask members of the group to display the clippings they collected during the past weeks and to look at those others brought in.

3. As group members arrive, involve them in playing Game 2 on the Connections Game Board: "Connections." The game may be played through several times until all members of the group are present. Playing this game may help people understand what interrelatedness and interdependence mean.

4. Play Game 6 on the Connections Game Board: "Steward-Neighbor." This game will give people a chance to think through some of the concepts that have been previously introduced and help them come to a contemporary understanding of the biblical images.

5. Provide group members with "Who Owns This Water?" page 16. Divide into four groups to write letters to the local newspaper editor in response to an article on water rights. The four groups are to take the following points of view from which to write:
- a Native American in North Dakota
- a South Dakota farmer
- an executive of an energy industry
- yourself

6. Play "Rainstorm" in order to call to mind sensations related to water. Everyone stands in a circle. The leader stands in the center and "conducts" the rainstorm as members of the group imitate the motion. The leader rubs his or her own hands together and turns around slowly in place until everyone is rubbing their own hands together. Then, coming around to the first person again, and while everyone is still rubbing hands, the leader starts snapping fingers and turns slowly, facing every person in turn until each one changes to finger-snapping. The next movement is hands slapping thighs. The final movement is slapping of thighs and stamping of feet—the crescendo of the storm. As with a thundershower, the volume decreases as the leader goes through each of the above steps in reverse until the last person rubbing their hands is silent.

6. Meditation experience with water: Ask people to sit in comfortable places with no books or purses in their hands or laps. Place a large bowl near each person. Have large jugs of water nearby for filling the bowls later.

Read the following in a thoughtful, prayerful manner,

taking plenty of time: "Sit in a comfortable position ...close your eyes...relax...take deep breaths... and think about water. Remember times when water has looked good to you. Remember times when water has *felt* good to you. When water has *tasted* good to you. Truly, water is a gift! Remember what water gives you...remember what God gives you with water. Water is a gift of Creation. With whom are you sharing water? With whom are you responsible for water? Now, we will take these jugs and pour water into our bowls. But first, enjoy the water...think about the water...use the water...feel the water...touch it to your face and arms. Now, open your eyes and silently pour the water into your bowls...using it and feeling it...in a quiet time of meditation...let us give thanks to God for water by saying aloud now why we are thankful for water...O God, we give thanks for water because _____
... O God, hear our prayers as we ask that _____
... O God, hear our prayers for forgiveness for _____. Your gifts in Creation show us how we are all connected with one another. Let us be stewards with each other and neighbors to each other. Amen."

7. Divide into groups of three or four to write what you feel is probable, possible, preferable with respect to water by the year 2000. Make a list for each of the three categories. Share them with the whole group.

8. In the small groups, choose some of the above items and list what you believe individuals might be doing in their own lifestyles to contribute toward that future. Share these with the whole group.

9. Ask group members to bring news clippings to post on the bulletin board for the next session.

MORE WAYS TO EXPLORE THE WATER WE DEPEND ON

1. Make banners related to the theme. Provide powdered tempera paints—red, blue, and yellow; small containers in which to mix paint, along with water and liquid soap; old brushes; the backs of old blueprints. People will enjoy using these materials and their imagination. You may want to play music that evokes water images as people paint.

2. Make a diagram or time line of what has happened to all the water that has been here since the beginning of Creation.

3. Look at frames 29, 58, 75, and 82 in "A Void of Desolation?" filmstrip. As a group, consider ways water is related to the land.

4. Pass out circles about 6 inches in diameter. Ask people to think of a life cycle or food chain and sketch it. Indicate on the circle ways that water pollution interrupts that cycle.

5. Choose one or more of the concerns related to water in your news clippings or in PRO-EARTH and identify the *local* factors behind these problems. How are *you* related to these problems? Some problems might include: fishing boundaries, acid rain, dams, drought, irrigation, draining salt marshes for commercial development, limited access to water, etc.

6. From the list of problems above or others you think of, identify ways that decisions by distant experts or legislators are affecting people locally.

7. Write to "International Drinking Water Supply and Sanitation Decade," United Nations Development Program, Division of Information, Room DC-1970, One U.N. Plaza, New York, NY 10017, for information and suggestions for action.

8. Make a list of all the professions you can think of in which people work with water. Place the following symbols beside them to help you to think about our attitudes towards these professions and towards water in general: Y=young people are encouraged to choose this occupation; PW=pays well; D=young people are discouraged from choosing this occupation; PP=pays poorly.

9. Use connecting toys such as circles, tinkertoys or pipecleaners. Label each part of these toys with the professions or names of people who care about water. Link them together to show how there are networks of people who care about water and who could work together for mutual benefit and for the benefit of all Creation. Some persons you may think of connecting are swimmers, fishers, septic tank workers, well-drillers, etc.

SESSION FOUR: LAND

PREPARATION

1. Read PRO-EARTH selections related to land.

2. Collect a quart bottle of "air," a pint of "swamp water," a bucket of soil, a container of sand and several rocks.

3. As described in Step 2 below, prepare Scripture posters and copies of the statements to be completed. Collect some pencils.

4. You may also wish to prepare newsprint charts on "Sunday Activities—Impact on the Land" and "Land Situations in the Filmstrip, 'A Void of Desolation?'"

5. Learn to play the Games 3 and 4 on the Connections Game Board. Prepare a playing area.

6. Obtain the filmstrip, projector, screen and cassette player. Set them up.

7. Obtain Bibles in contemporary versions, paper and pencils.

EXPERIENCING LAND

1. As people come in, they can walk around the display of the quart of air, the pint of swamp water, the bucket of soil, the container of sand and the rocks. Ask them to make price tags for each item to help them think about the value of land.

2. Write out the following passages on posters: Leviticus 25:2b, 25:23, 25:55, 26:3-4; Psalm 23:1, 24:1; Joshua 24:12a-13.

3. Make copies of several of the following statements for people to complete as they come:
- When I see fences, I think . . .
- A "NO TRESPASSING" sign makes me wonder. . .
- When I see cut trees, I feel. . .
- Seeing a driver toss a bottle into the bushes makes me think . . .
- Cairns make me think of . . .
- I feel. . .when I see graffiti on rocks.
- When I see plants and trees in a nursery, I wonder. . .
- When I see people taking short-cuts, I feel . . .
- Hazardous wastes seem . . .
- Pesticides encourage. . .
- I wonder. . .about paved parking lots.
- Litter makes me feel . . .
- Hikers might . . .
- Septic systems make me think . . .
- When there are no fences, I feel . . .

After members of the group have completed these statements or others you might think of, ask them to share what they have written with a partner. Such sharing gives people a chance to give more consideration to the land than they usually do in their daily lives.

4. As a whole group, take a typical day's schedule—perhaps a Sunday—and list on the left-hand side of a piece of newsprint everything the group members do on that day. To the right of each item, list the impact that activity has on the land. If the group is large, this activity might work better in smaller groups.

Recalling our activities and thinking about their impact increases our awareness of the implications of our lifestyles.

5. Using the Connections Game Board, play Game 3, "Obstacle-Solution," and Game 4, "Individual or Group Influence?" Instructions are with each game.

6. Watch the filmstrip, "A Void of Desolation?" Before you show it, ask group members to be ready to list all the situations they see that affect the land. After watching the filmstrip, ask them to form small groups and discuss how ordinary citizens might relate to those situations. What would the roles of experts be?

7. Ask group members to read silently all the scriptures posted on the wall and all of Leviticus 25. Then ask them to write an ad—or perhaps a poem—about what it means to them to sell property. Ask people to share what they have written as a closing meditation.

8. Remind the group to continue to bring in newspaper clippings related to water and land issues, and to continue reading the text.

MORE WAYS TO EXPLORE THE LAND WE LIVE ON

1. Using ideas in the readings from PRO-EARTH, create a litany in which the partnership between God and humanity is renewed.

2. As a group, write a prayer about *dominion, partnership* and *caretaking*.

3. Divide into two groups. Ask the members of one group to complete the following sentence: "The economics of land requires us to _____." Members of the other group complete: "Technology forces us to _____." As a total group, read each statement and identify the one(s) with which you agree. What makes you disagree with the others?

4. The following situations are to be acted out spontaneously by four people. Two will be trying to sell a piece of land and two will be trying to buy that land. The rest of the group acts as the audience and tries to identify what factors are motivating the actors and whether they are appropriate or not.

Situations: selling your land to a gravel company to use as a rock quarry; selling woodland that is not bringing in any income; buying two lots and planning to build a house on only one for more privacy; selling swamp land to a real estate developer.

5. List the following on a chart: artifacts, rocks, animals, flowers (add more that you think of). Beside each item, make two columns: "It is OK to _____" and "It is not OK to _____." Write your answers for each item in that column.

6. Using the Connections Game Board, play Game 5, "Possible, Probable, Preferable."

7. Talk about places in your community where people have dumped garbage. Your group may want to go out together to find out where this is going on. When you find them, ask police or health inspectors whether these are appropriate dumps.

SESSION FIVE: SHARING THE RESPONSIBILITY

PREPARATION

1. Collect enough children's building kits or Lego

toys so that everyone will have enough to work with.
   2. Collect paper, pencils, crayons or markers and Bibles.
   3. Prepare copies of "This Land is Home to Us," page 22 and "How to Make Hard Decisions about Energy," page 64.
   4. Practice the game "Knots."
   5. Read the text. Assign leadership responsibilities.

EXPERIENCING OUR INTERDEPENDENCE

   1. As people arrive, ask them to build one of the following items from the Lego toys: a machine that will prevent plant diseases, a machine that will turn on the water faucet, a machine that will get people to work together. Display all the machines and ask people to explain how they work. Some questions to think about:
   a) Does it destroy anything?
   b) Is it as effective as people?
   c) How does it benefit the earth?
   d) How does it benefit humanity?
   e) Does it take over a human task?
   f) Is the fuel used comparable to or greater than the good it does?
   g) What would it cost to manufacture this machine?

If you choose not to use building kits or Lego toys the group can draw the machines on paper. Another possibility for making these machines is human sculpture. Six to ten persons can produce a machine using the shapes they make with their bodies, connecting and moving as needed. Ask the above questions about these human sculpture machines.

   2. Each group that designed a machine should get together now with crayons, markers and paper and dream up an advertisement for their machine. They already know its strengths and weaknesses, but they need to produce an advertisement if people are going to buy it.

Share the ads. Then each design group talks about the ethical and economic dilemmas or problems they faced.

   3. Provide copies of "This Land is Home to Us," and "How to Make Hard Decisions about Energy." Ask the group: Which of these guidelines were taken into account in the decisions that were made in "This Land is Home to Us?"

Divide into three groups to identify:
   a) what can individuals do to make this land situation different?
   b) what can groups do to make it different?
   c) what can institutions like the church do to make it different?

   4. Read Matthew 25:21 aloud. Ask group members to think about and list: What can I do individually, with a group and as a part of an institution like the church if I am trying to live out of the image of the faithful servant?

Ask people who wish to share what they have written to read their list. The group responds by repeating the words of Matthew 25:21.

   5. Play "Knots" as a closing activity.

Ask group members (if there are more than ten, have more than one group), to stand in a circle, then reach out and take hold of two different people's hands—people *not* standing next to them. Now, without dropping hands, untangle the knots so that the circle forms itself again. How was this untangling similar to the biblical images of the faithful servant, the neighbor, the steward? Ask how the experience of playing "Knots" is similar to each of the above biblical images. Reflect, too, on how it was similar to the way we live interdependently when we care for God's earth.

MORE WAYS TO EXPLORE OUR SHARED RESPONSIBILITY

   1. Using the Connections Game Board, play Game 7, "Dominoes," and Game 8, "Memorizing Connections."

   2. Using the actual objects, pictures of them, or cards with a description of these things, arrange on a continuum from "appropriate technology" to "inappropriate technology": an electric toothbrush, a push lawn mower, nuclear energy for electricity production, pesticides, a toothpick, a hot water bottle, a portable space heater, an iron, a hair dryer, a clothes dryer, an exercise bicycle, black plastic bags for gardeners, compost, homemade scarecrow devices, a garbage compactor, a bundle of old newspapers. Think of more if you wish. The group can write ads for these items to show how our popular culture influences us.

   3. By now it may be possible for a group to act out what "neighbor" means in relation to land and water. Ask another group to act out what "steward" means in relation to land or water.

GAMES

PREPARING THE CONNECTIONS GAME BOARD

Cover the Game Board with clear contact paper. That will protect the surface for longer life and let players write directly on the board with water-soluble markers. After the board has been marked up according to each game's directions (for example, Game 2 suggests marking the game pieces with categories) it can be wiped off with a damp cloth.

Make multiple copies of the game so that there is always a twelve-square section available for each player. Or make enough copies of the Game Board and game directions so that everyone can take them home to play with other people—a good way to spread news about the concerns we're talking about.

Game 1: "Twenty Questions."

Look at all the words and phrases on the game board. Choose one, and without telling anyone what it is, say to the group, "The phrase or word I am thinking of relates to land" (or air, water, energy, stewardship, etc.)." Then the group asks you "yes" or "no" questions to guess which one you have chosen.

Game 2: "Connections."

Cut the boards apart so there are "playing cards" consisting of twelve squares: four squares by three squares. Give each person a card. Look at other peoples' cards; is there anything written on the outer edge of your card that connects in some way with an item on the outer edge of another person's card?

Now, look at least four items in a row that have a clear connection to one of these five categories: air, water, land, food, or energy. Write the category on the card (like X and O in tic-tac-toe). If you can find five in a row, all the better! The rows can be straight or diagonal. Mark as many rows of relationships as you can, using as many categories as you can connect with your items. After everyone has finished marking their connections, share your connections and tell how you see them connected. If there is disagreement, try to arrive at a consensus.

Game 3: "Obstacle-Solution."

Using any of the words and phrases on any of the cards (or others, if you wish), the leader calls out one word or phrase. Group members each have a twelve-square playing card and if, on their card, they have either an obstacle or a solution to what was called out, they mark it. Players should try to see as many connections as possible and to mark as many of their squares as possible. In the end, players may tell why they marked their items. If there is disagreement, try for consensus. The leader may wish to ask players to try to get four items in a row marked as either an obstacle or a solution, rather than simply marking as many as possible.

Game 4: "Individual or Group Influence?"

Give each player a twelve-square playing card. Flip a coin. "Heads" means "individual." "Tails" means "group." Players are to mark one item on their card that can be affected by an *individual* or by a *group*. The object is to mark four items in a row. You may want to change the object to, say, four "individual" marks in a row or four "group" marks in a row. Ask group members to share what they have marked in the end. If there is disagreement, players can discuss the issue until there is consensus about whether an individual could affect the item or whether a group's intervention would be necessary.

Game 5: "Possible, Probable, Preferable."

Give each person a twelve-square playing card. At random, call out "possible!" or "probable!" or "preferable!" As you call them out, players are to mark one item on their card with the word called out: "pos," "prob" or "pref." When someone gets four "pref's" in a row, stop the game and share the markings. If no one gets four "pref's" in a row, stop the game when someone finally has all their items marked.

Game 6: "Steward-Neighbor."

Give each player a twelve-square playing card. Flip a coin and call out "steward!" if it is heads and "neighbor!" if it is tails. Persons are to mark one item each time "steward" or "neighbor" is called if they see a way in which one of their items is connected to that biblical image. After a player has marked four in a row or someone's card is completely marked, share why you have marked the cards.

Game 7: "Dominoes."

Cut the cards apart so that there are two cards connected, like a domino. Deal out an equal number of domino cards to each person. One player begins by laying down any card. From that point, moving clockwise, players connect one of their items to one end or the other of the line of dominoes. If they do not have a connection, they pass until their next turn. Players should explain and agree about the connections they make.

Game 8: "Memorizing Connections."

Cut apart all the squares and turn them face down on a table. Each player turns up two cards, looks at them and if they connect in some way that the whole group agrees upon, he or she removes them. If they do *not* connect, the cards are turned back over in their original position. Each player does this in turn until connections have been made for all cards.

YOUTH LEADER'S GUIDE
by Fred Coulter

TO THE YOUTH LEADER:
It's been my experience that the big unspoken question behind any youth group's gathering is, "What's in this for *me*?" The issues raised in PRO-EARTH are not likely to draw a standing-room-only crowd. It's not easy to interpret these crucial environmental issues in terms of a teenager's everyday life and hopes. Yet that's the task you've taken on.

The activities outlined in this guide are discussion-starters only. The discussion itself may have to do with a particular selection from PRO-EARTH, or perhaps an environmental or eco-justice issue in your own community. Before the group meets, put on your "eco-justice lenses" and find an issue in the local newspaper or check out what the neighbors are talking about. You might even ask the kids if they have heard environmental concerns about the neighborhood they live in.

I see this discussion on caring for God's earth as a one-time evening activity or perhaps a weekend retreat. The discussion starters are self-contained units — they do not need to be part of a series of discussions on the environment, which most kids I know would avoid.

Just giving the youth a chance to talk together about these issues is very important. No consensus is necessary. The discussion that evolves may be full of "wrong" attitudes or negative perceptions of how much good one person can do. My goal would simply be to raise the youth's awareness of these issues; some of them may be threatening to teenagers who are very much aware of the job market they face. Let them know they can talk with each other about these ideas without being put down. In the end, they may begin to think, "This stuff *is* important to me. This *does* have to do with my life."

1. CREATION, GOD AND YOU

Begin by giving each person a piece of paper and a pencil. Take them outside and have them list all the things they notice about nature—what nature does, what nature is like. (Examples: the great variety of colors, the intricacy of plant structure, the way the sun heats the earth and enables life to exist, and so on.)

After fifteen or twenty minutes, have the group come together again and ask each person to share his or her findings with the rest of the group.

The next part of the exercise is to be used as a take-off to find out what Scripture has to say about the God who created it all. Ask the group to describe the most scenic spot they have ever visited, or where they think is the most beautiful place in the world. Or ask them what it is about Creation that amazes them most.

Then, have different people read the following passages: Genesis 1:4, 1:26, 2:7; Romans 8:21-23; Hebrews 11:3.

After each passage is read, ask someone to briefly state in his or her own words what the basic idea of the passage is.

Lead the group in a discussion of God's nature as it is expressed through Creation. Suggest to the group that the Scripture they just heard and other Scripture they think about can be the basis from which to think about and answer the following questions:

1. What are some things we know about God upon observing God's creation? Can you list some of God's attributes?

2. Is Creation an extension of God, or is Creation something separate from God?

3. In the beginning, God looked at Creation and said it was good. Is it still good?

4. What do you think was the purpose of Creation?

5. Is Creation still going on? Is God still involved in Creation? Explain.

6. How does what we know about God through Creation help us to trust God?

7. How does nature speak to you in a personal way?

8. How do you *use* nature in your life every day? Are there any ways you think you might be abusing nature?

2. CREATION MEDITATION

This meditation is excellent for those who are new at meditation exercises. Ask the kids to sit on the floor in a circle with their legs crossed. Place a cup of soil and a cup of water before each one. Ask them to note where

---

The Rev. Fred Coulter is minister of First Congregational Church, Ledyard, CT.

the water and soil have been placed, then ask them to close their eyes and relax. They should systematically relax their muscles from their head to their toes.

Explain that you will be reading verses from Genesis and that you want them to use their imaginations in giving God thanks for Creation. When you read the Scripture, and then the words for meditation, read *very* slowly, with pauses between each thought.

Read Genesis 1:1 and 3, "In the beginning God created the heavens and the earth"; "And God said, 'Let there be light'; and there was light." Then say, "Thank God for light. What if you lived in darkness? Picture the face of someone you dearly love—a friend, a parent, a boyfriend or girlfriend. Now, let the face melt away into darkness. What if you lived in darkness? Thank God for light!" (Keep your eyes closed).

Read Genesis 1:6, "And God said, 'Let there be a firmament in the midst of the waters, and let it separate the waters from the waters.'" Then say, "Do you take water for granted? What if we ran out of it? Taste a few drops of water from the cup. Keep them in your mouth. Appreciate them for a moment. All of life depends on water. Thank God for water!"

Read Genesis 1:9, "And God said, 'Let the dry land appear.' And it was so." Then say, "Do you take the earth for granted? Reach out and touch the soil. Rub it between your fingers. Smell it. What if we should pollute all of the earth's soil? Could we exist? Thank God for soil!"

Read Genesis 1:14, "And God said, 'Let there be lights in the firmament of the heavens to separate the day from the night; and let them be for signs and for seasons and for days and years.'"

Then, have different people read the following passages:

Genesis 1:4, "And God saw that the light was good; and God separated the light from the darkness."

Genesis 1:26, "Then God said, "Let us make humankind in our image, after our likeness; and let them have dominion over the fish of the sea, and over the birds of the air, and over the cattle, and over all the earth, and over every creeping thing that creeps upon the earth."

Genesis 2:7, "Then God the Sovereign One formed a human creature of dust from the ground, and breathed into the creature's nostrils the breath of life; and the human creature became a living being."

Romans 8:21-23, "Because the creation itself will be set free from its bondage to decay and obtain the glorious liberty of the children of God. "We know that the whole creation has been groaning in travail together until now; and not only the creation, but we ourselves, who have first fruits of the Spirit, groan inwardly as we wait for adoption as children [of God], the redemption of our bodies." Hebrews 11:3, "By faith we understand that the world was created by the word of God, so that what is seen was made out of things which do not appear."

After each passage is read, ask someone to briefly state in their own words what the basic idea of the passage is. Then say, "What if the seasons never changed? What if it were always winter? Picture your yard at home with no flowers, no leaves on the trees, no green bushes—not just for a few months out of the year, but for the whole year long. Thank God for the seasons!"

Say, "Lay back on the floor now and completely relax while continuing to thank God for creation." (It is good to change positions for the sake of comfort and relaxation.)

Read Genesis 1:20, "And God said, 'Let the waters bring forth swarms of living creatures, and let birds fly above the earth across the firmament of the heavens.'" Then say, "Thank God for birds. They teach us to soar. Picture yourself as a gliding seagull. Imagine that you are flying out over the ocean. You approach the shoreline and see the water lapping the shore. Now fly away and see as high or as far as you would like. Fly back to land now. You are a gull walking along the shore. Thank God for birds."

Read Genesis 1:24, "And God said, 'Let the earth bring forth living creatures according to their kinds: cattle and creeping things and beasts of the earth according to their kinds.' And it was so." Then say, "Now, picture yourself as some kind of animal. Any kind. What kind of animal are you? Where do you live? What is it like there today? What are you doing? Thank God for animals!"

Read Genesis 1:26-27, "Then God said 'Let us make humankind in our image, after our likeness; and let them have dominion over the fish of the sea, and over the birds of the air, and over the cattle, and over all the earth, and over every creeping thing that creeps upon the earth.' So God created humankind in God's own image, in the image of God was the human being created; male and female God created them." Then say, "Thank God for *you*! Do you appreciate yourself? Keep your eyes closed. Run your hand through your hair. Is it fine or coarse? Now, touch your ear. Run your finger along its edge. Feel its shape. Now, without opening your eyes, put your hand in front of your face. Try to remember what it looks like. Try to picture how many lines run across your palm. Try to feel how the veins run across the back

---

Biblical quotations are from An Inclusive Language Lectionary: Readings for Year A, copyrighted © 1983 by the Division of Education and Ministry of the National Council of the Churches of Christ in the U.S.A., and is used by permission.

of your hand. Now, open your eyes and look closely at your hand, and thank God for you."

"Let us pray. Dear God, we thank you for all your Creation. Help us to never take it for granted. In Jesus' spirit. Amen."

(To the leader: All questions above and the entire meditation should be adapted to your own geographical area.

3. LETTER TO AMOS

The following is good after a study of the Old Testament book of Amos. Pass out copies of this "open letter" to Amos and discuss the arguments presented. Some suggested questions for discussion follow.

Dear Mr. Amos:

Your intemperate criticisms of the merchants of Bethel show that you have little understanding of the operations of a modern business economy. You appear not to understand that a business person is entitled to a profit. A cobbler sells shoes to make money, as much as he or she can. A banker lends money to get a return on his or her loan. These are not charitable enterprises. Without profits, a tradesperson cannot stay in business.

Your slander reveals a lack of appreciation for the progress of the past few decades. The beautiful public buildings and private homes are a proud monument to the wealth of our civilization. Increasing our contacts with foreign lands adds to the cultural opportunities open to our citizens. Our military strength makes us the envy of peoples already swallowed up by their enemies.

Despite the great gains during Jereboam II's reign, there is some poverty. This we admit. But is it fair to blame the government for the inability of some people to compete? You say that the peasants were cheated out of their lands. Not so! They sold their property, or in some cases it was sold for back taxes. Some peasants put up the land as collateral on a loan, then failed to meet the payments. No one was cheated. The transactions to which you refer were entirely legal. Had you taken the trouble to investigate the facts, your conclusions would have been more accurate.

The real reason for poverty is lack of initiative. People who get ahead in this world work hard, take risks, overcome obstacles. Dedication and determination are the keys to success. Opportunities don't knock: they are created by imagination and industry.

Our success can be an inspiration to the poor. If we can make it, they can too. With the growth of business, Israel grows. More jobs, better pay and increased opportunity for everyone. The old saying contains more than a germ of truth: what's good for General Chariots is good for the country.

Yours for Israel,

Discussion questions:

1. Evaluate the merchant's arguments in the light of justice. At what points do the business people convince you? When do they fail to convince you?
2. Suppose this letter were written today. How would you react? Where do the rights of the individual stop? Can justice be administered without striking a balance between individual rights and the rights of the community?
3. What *about* justice? Just *us*? Just *U.S.*? Just *who*?

4. TWENTY-FIRST CENTURY

Future shock is something that affects all of us, and this discussion can help your youth start preparing for the future.

Begin with a devotional reflection on Revelation 21:1-5: "Then I saw a new heaven and a new earth; for the first heaven and the first earth had passed away, and the sea was no more. And I saw the holy city, new Jerusalem, coming down out of heaven from God, prepared as a bride adorned for her husband; and I heard a great voice from the throne saying, "Behold the dwelling of God is with human beings. God will dwell with them, and they shall be God's people, and God will be with them. God will wipe away every tear from their eyes, and death shall be no more, neither shall there be mourning nor crying nor pain any more, for the former things have passed away.

"And the one who sat upon the throne said, 'Behold, I make all things new,' to which was added, 'Write this, for these words are trustworthy and true.'"

Talk about what God has planned for the future—a new heaven and a new earth; no more tears, no more death; no more grief, crying, pain, etc. That is all great, but what about the world we live in now? What is going to happen in the next few years?

Give each of the youth a list like the one below:

Travel/transportation	Household gadgets
Government	Social relations
Work	Economy (money)
Recreation	Foreign relations
Housing/architecture	Outer space
Entertainment	Music
Personal items	Families
Church/religion	Medicine
Food	Funerals
Clothes	Sports
Education	Art
Environment	Journalism

Divide into small groups and have each group select five or six areas of interest. Then give each group 45 minutes to brainstorm or fantasize the world they would like to see in the twenty-first century. Give them poster-size paper so they can illustrate, graphically or symbolically, what this world may be like. Display all the posters at the end of the session and have each group explain what they have shown.

5. PAUL'S LETTER TO THE NORTH AMERICANS

This is an activity that causes both the youth and leaders to reflect on their present lives and helps them get a feeling for Paul's letters to the churches.

Have each youth write a letter to himself or herself from "Paul," praising and admonishing themselves on their lifestyle. It's important to praise as well as admonish! Give them about twenty minutes, then let them break into groups of three or four and share their letters.

Or use a specific passage like Ephesians 6:10-24. Hand out copies of the passage and ask the youth to rewrite it to themselves. Or have small groups compose a letter to the whole youth group evaluating what the youth group is or is not doing.

6. EARTHLY COLLAGE

Divide the group into smaller groups of three or four people. Hand each group a stack of magazines and newspapers. (Magazines heavy on advertisements are best.) Ask each group to pretend that they are Martians who have spent several days observing Earthlings' habits. To illustrate what Earthlings are like, they have brought back to Mars photographic evidence (pictorial advertisements without words).

Each group then tears out advertisements (no words—cross out the brand names) and pastes together a collage of what they see. The first impression you get from a pictorial advertisement without the attached brand names and flowery phrases can provide quite a social and often hilarious commentary on our priorities and style of living!

7. REAL WORLD SIMULATION GAME

The following game can be used effectively prior to a discussion on poverty throughout the world, on the use of natural resources, international relations or any number of relevant subjects. The game involves a realistic situation of survival centering around the grain production capability and food needs of various countries.

The game involves seven small groups of people (it can be adapted to a different number of groups). Each group is a country with designated grain production and grain needs per month—and also a monthly income.

Materials needed:

1. Fifteen plus cups of grain (unpopped popcorn or whatever can be conveniently measured and handled)
2. Three rolls of pennies
3. Eight plastic measuring cups with graduations to one-eighth cup. The leader gets a cup and each country gets one cup.
4. Seven 3x5 "weather cards"—three blank, three reading "drought" or "flood," and one reading "bumper crop."
5. Eight copies of the World Situation Fact Sheet—one for each country and the leader.

Instructions

1. GOAL: Your purpose is to survive as a nation in whatever way you choose: beg (call it foreign aid), borrow or buy.

2. PREPARATION: You will have ten minutes in which to study the Fact Sheet and elect the following officers:

a) A President to lead the group in deciding his or her country's policies and to negotiate with other countries that come to beg or borrow or buy. The President may not leave the country group.

b) Ambassadors to negotiate for their country. The group may elect more than one ambassador if they feel the need.

c) A Treasurer to keep track of and guard the grain and money.

World Situation Fact Sheet				
Country	*Direct Trading Countries	Monthly Grain Production	Monthly Grain Needs	Monthly Gross National Income
Canada	All Countries	2 Cups	1/2 Cup	3¢
China	Japan, Great Britain, Canada ONLY	2 1/2 Cups	3 Cups	1¢
Great Britain	all but the Soviet Union	1/2 Cup	3/4 Cup	3¢
India	all but China	3/4 Cup	2 Cups	1¢
Japan	all but the Soviet Union	1/4 Cup	1 Cup	4¢
Soviet Union	India, Canada, United States ONLY	2 1/2 Cups	1 1/2 Cups	2¢
United States	all but China	2 1/2 Cups	1 1/4 Cups	5¢

* Trading with countries that you're not allowed to trade with DIRECTLY may be traded with through a neutral country acting as an intermediary. A neutral country is one that can trade directly with the countries that want to negotiate.

Method of Play

1. The game is played in time periods of one month, six months total, of ten minutes each month. Each month, the country will receive a monthly income and grain quota. At the end of each month, the country will have taken away from it its monthly consumption of grain. The job of the group and those elected is to see that, in the ten minutes alloted, their country will have enough grain at the end of the month to equal the consumption that will be taken away.

2. When time is called at the end of the month, all play must stop; all inter-country communication must cease; all players must return to their respective countries.

3. At the beginning of each month except the first month, each country's President will draw a weather card. A blank card indicates good weather and no change in grain production. "Flood" and "drought" cards mean your grain production is cut in half that month; "bumper crop" means you have one cup extra (for large grain producers) or one half cup extra (for small grain producers) that month. Make three good weather cards, one "bumper crop" card, and three "drought" or "flood" cards.

4. If a country needs to buy grain from another country, their ambassador must negotiate the amount. The cost of grain is one cent per half-cup.

5. Each country is given their amount of money each month as indicated by the far right column, "Monthly Gross National Income," on the World Situation Fact Sheet. The leader of the game distributes the money at the beginning of each month.

Starvation

If you do not have enough grain at the end of any month to meet your country's needs as indicated on the Fact Sheet, your country starves and is out of the game.

TO THE LEADER:

Most of the tradings instructions are included on the World Situation Fact Sheet. However you need to keep a few other things in mind:

1. Have all the supplies distributed to each team before the "preparation" period begins in order to save confusion.

2. Make sure all the taking of monthly consumption and giving of monthly production and income is fully completed between each monthly time-period before another time period is begun.

3. Between each time period, collect the "weather" cards and re-shuffle them and have the leaders of each country pick them at random. This, too, should be done before a new time period has begun.

4. It is important that the leader of the game refrain as much as possible from giving additional instructions or answering questions once the game is in process. This will give the players chance to take more initiative in tackling the task without constantly depending on the leader of the game to guide them towards a successful conclusion.

5. If your situation calls for a different number of countries than seven, you will need to make up a new World Situation Fact Sheet. In setting up a different situation, make sure you have the total grain and money needed. This will allow (at least theoretically) the survival of every country.

The games in the Youth Leader's Guide were adapted from IDEAS, published by Youth Specialties, El Cajon, CA, edited by Wayne Rice and Mike Yaconelli. Sources for the ideas are: "God, Creation and You," Anna Hobbs; "Creation Meditation," Douglas Iben; "Letter to Amos," Homer Erekson; "Twenty-First Century," Jimmie L. Hancock; "Paul's Letter to the North Americans," Kris Yotter; "Earthly Collage," Glenn Miller; "Real World Game," W. Clarence Schett.

BIBLIOGRAPHY

GLOBAL ENVIRONMENT ISSUES

America's Energy: Reports from The Nation on 100 years of Struggles for Democratic Control of our Resources. Edited by Robert Engler. New York: Pantheon, 1981. Paper, $7.95.

This anthology of articles from *The Nation* magazine, arranged into chapters on coal, electric power, oil, nuclear power and alternative sources of energy, gives an historical perspective on how energy resources have been viewed over a hundred years—and how they have been treated in the political arena. The articles illustrate a pattern which explains the failure of government to produce a truly national energy policy and program.

Berry, Wendell. *The Gift of Good Land.* San Francisco: North Point Press, 1981.

Using specific examples, the author documents the interrelationships between human individuals, land, weather, cropping systems and the community. Berry is a poet, teacher, philosopher and farmer.

———. *The Unsettling of America.* New York: Avon Books, 1978. Paper, $6.95.

A controversial cultural and technical critique of mass machine agriculture in America, its ideological roots and self-destructive character as well as alternative options.

Brown, Lester R. *State of the World: 1985.* Washington, D.C.: World Watch Institute, 1985. Paper, $8.95.

This is a report on the progress of the people of the world towards a sustainable society. It is directed towards the general reader and links together pollution, hunger, health and economic development often discussed as separate issues in a way that is instructive.

Brown, Michael. *Living Waste: The Poisoning of America by Toxic Chemicals.* New York: Washington Square Press, 1981. Paper, $3.95.

This journalist, whose stories in 1978 about the Love Canal crisis brought the problem of improperly-buried toxic chemicals to public attention, here discusses that site and moves on to recount the impact of poorly safeguarded dumpsites on other communities. The efforts of government and of industry to dodge the cleanup issue is made painfully clear.

Bull, David. *A Growing Problem: Pesticides and the Third World Poor.* London: Oxfam, 1982. Available from the Institute for Food and Development Policy, 1885 Mission Street, San Francisco, CA 94104. Paper, $9.95.

This work focuses on the human suffering which results from the uncontrolled sale and use of pesticides in the third world, and the benefits of a well-integrated program of pest management.

Byron, William. *The Causes of World Hunger.* New York: Paulist Press, 1984. Paper, $8.95.

Carson, Rachel. *Silent Spring.* (originally published in 1962) New York: Fawcett, 1978. Paper, $2.95.

This work broke new ground in bringing together little-known scientific evidence on the side-effects of chemical sprays used in agriculture. It brought the author a storm of criticism from those within the pesticide industry and sparked the environmental movement of the 1960's.

This bibliography is drawn from annotated bibliographies compiled by Elizabeth Mellon by the Women's Division, United Methodist General Board of Global Ministries and J. Benton Rhoades, Director of Agricultural Missions, National Council of the Churches of Christ. Friendship Press is grateful for their permission to use this material.

The Coalition for Appalachian Ministry. *Erets: Land—The Church and Appalachian Land Issues.* 1984. Available for $3.00 plus postage and handling from C.A.M., P.O. Box 159, Amesville, OH 45711.

This is empowering work for those beginning to sense the links between biblical faith and land use and abuse. A paper by theologian Walter Brueggemann discusses the biblical use of the words land and earth (both are *erets* in Hebrew). Also included is David Liden's synthesis of the Appalachian Land Ownership study, excerpted in PRO-EARTH.

Cogswell, James A., *No Place Left Called Home.* New York: Friendship Press, 1983.

Stories of uprooted people throughout the world explore the causes of refugee situations. How can Christians move beyond sympathy to heal the brokeness of people torn from their roots?

Commoner, Barry. *The Closing Circle: Confronting the Environmental Crisis.* Woodstock, NY: Beekman Publications, 1973. $14.95. New York: Bantam Books. Paper, $3.95.

A deeply-respected landmark work which some call the best book on ecology ever written. Briefly, clearly and rigorously, Commoner, an environmental scientist and educator, shows how technology's conversion of natural cycles into dead-end waste lies at the root of environmental stress.

———. *The Poverty of Power: Energy and the Economic Crisis.* New York: Knopf, 1976. $10.00.

A fine general book on the overall shape of our society as viewed in the light of the "energy crisis." The author presents the basic information and explains the technological dimensions of the problem in a lively and lucid way.

deBell, Garret, ed. *The New Environmental Handbook.* Andover, MA: Brick House, 1980. Paper, $5.95.

This handbook brings together students, scientists, writers and others to focus on some of the major problems and suggest action that can be taken now in any community.

Eckholm, Erik P., *Losing Ground.* New York. W. W. Norton and Company, 1976. Paper, $6.95.

This book documents the global extent of ecological stress on the land and its threat to future world food supplies and to the quality of life of rural populations. Its weakness is in its pointing to over-population and to slash-and-burn agriculture as the root causes of the problem without adequate analysis of the role that global agribusiness plays.

Engler, Robert. *The Brotherhood of Oil: Energy Policy and the Public Interest.* Chicago: University of Chicago Press, 1977. $12.50.

In this work, the author seeks to show how oil corporations, in collaboration with governmental agencies, fix the boundaries of energy policy alternatives over virtually the entire globe. The material on the role of the Department of the Interior in partnership with industry has particular relevance to Native American questions.

Epstein, Samuel S. and others. *Hazardous Waste in America: Our Number-One Environmental Crisis.* San Francisco: The Sierra Club, 1983. Paper, $12.95. Order from Random House.

This work covers the topic of hazardous waste from the ecological, medical, legal and political angles. It gives the nature, composition, toxic properties and sources of these wastes, a history of federal legislation and legal actions taken on hazardous wastes.

Freudenberg, Nicholas. *Not in Our Backyards! Community Action for Health and the Environment.* Forward by Lois Marie Gibbs. New York: Monthly Review Press, 1984. Paper, $10.00.

The Global 2000 Report to the President: Entering the Twenty-first Century. Washington, D.C.: U.S. Government Printing Office, 1980. Vol. I, Summary Report is available in paper — New York: Penguin, 1982. $10.00.

This report was originated by the Carter Administration. It gathers a great deal of data to reveal the serious situation we are in regarding the steady depletion of resources and deterioration of the world's natural systems.

Lappe, Frances Moore. *Diet for a Small Planet.* New York: Ballantine Books, 1975. Paper, $2.75.

This book calls into question our stewardship of one of the earth's most precious commodities: food. Lappe not only questions the contradictions in the American agricultural system and the national diet, but suggests solutions to the American tendency to eat more than our share of the earth's protein.

Lappe, Frances M. and Joseph Collins. *Food First: Beyond the Myth of Scarcity.* New York: Ballantine, 1979. Paper, $2.95.

This book explains how the causes of hunger are to be found in the legacy of colonialism, which destroyed traditional agriculture, and in the domination of food production and distribution by multinational corporations. Its point: that local needs should come before profitmaking.

———. *World Hunger: Ten Myths.* Revised edition, San Francisco: Institute for Food and Development Policy, 1979. Paper, $2.95. Order from the Institute, 1885 Mission Street, San Francisco, CA 94103.

Nader, Ralph and John Abbotts. *The Risk of Atomic Energy.* New York: W. W. Norton, 1979.

There are a number of like books written to scare us, though they also lack constructive purpose (e.g., *Meltdown; The Day We Almost Lost Detroit*). This book may scare us too, but its intent is to arouse us to join with other people for concerned action.

Pawlick, Thomas. *A Killing Rain: The Global Threat of Acid Precipitation.* (A Sierra Club Book) New York: Random House, 1984. $14.95.

The author reports on how acid rain endangers aquatic life in lakes, human health, forests and crops, and the failure of the U.S. government to set strict pollution standards for coal-burning power plants.

A Quiet Revolution: The United Nations Convention on the Law of the Sea. New York: United Nations, 1984. $6.50. Available from Unipub, Box 1222, Ann Arbor, MI 48106. Price includes postage and handling. Order No. 4052-UN63/5/7.

The key features of the Convention are described: its emphasis on ecology, scientific research in the sea, mining, creation of the International Sea-Bed Authority. The U.S. has still failed to sign this convention.

Regenstein, Lewis. *America the Poisoned.* Washington, D.C.: Acropolis, 1982. Paper, $8.95.

This work demonstrates how America and much of the world have been poisoned by the relentless use of toxic substances released into the environment.

Samuels, Mike and Hal ZinaBennett. *Well Body, Well Earth: The Sierra Club Environmental Health Source*

Book. San Francisco: Sierra Club Books, 1983. Paper, $12.95. Order from Random House.

This work is based on the premise that the earth is a living entity and that its functions are closely interconnected with human health. The many causes of environmental "disease" are discussed, along with their effects on human health. Appendix includes tables on toxic substances, a directory of political action groups and a bibliography.

Shanks, Bernard. *This Land is Your Land: The Struggle to Save America's Public Lands*. (A Sierra Club book) New York: Random House, 1984. $19.95.

The author calls for sweeping reform of the government's management of public lands.

Simon, Arthur. *Bread For the World*. Revised ed. Grand Rapids: Eerdmans, 1984. Paper, $5.95.

Arthur Simon is executive director of Bread for the World, a national Christian citizen's movement formed ten years ago to make governmental policies more responsive to hungry people in the U.S. and abroad. This edition takes into account the economic and political climate of the 1980's. The "What can I do?" study questions make the work a widely-used discussion resource.

Van Strum, Carol. *A Bitter Fog: Herbicides and Human Rights*. San Francisco: Sierra Club Books, 1982. $14.95. Order from Random House.

Van Strum helped found the Oregon-based Citizens Against Toxic Sprays. Her book is an impassioned, thoroughly-researched work that starts with the story of her own children being sprayed and then moves on to details of damage to crops, sicknesses from contaminated water, miscarriages, incidents in Vietnam and her own group's battle against Forest Service, EPA and chemical firms.

Ward, Barbara and Rene Dubos. *Only One Earth: The Care and Maintenance of a Small Planet*. New York: W. W. Norton and Co., Inc. 1972. $6.95.

Commissioned by the United Nations Conference on the Human Environment and prepared with the help of a committee of consultants from fifty-eight countries, this often-moving statement looks at ecological problems in their social, political and economic dimensions.

Who's Poisoning America? Corporate Polluters and their Victims in the Chemical Age. San Francisco: Sierra Club Books, 1980. Paper, $12.95. Order from Random House.

Edited by Ralph Nader and others, this book for the general reader presents seven cases of chemical pollution examined by local journalists. Included are cases of cattle feed containing PCB's, mine wastes in Lake Superior, Love Canal. The final chapter has thoughtful recommendations for what people can do to ensure the accountability of those who commit "chemical crimes."

RELIGIOUS, CULTURAL AND THEOLOGICAL ISSUES

Avila, Charles. *Ownership, Early Christian Teaching*. Orbis, New York 1981. Paper, $9.95.

An anthology and commentary on early church teachings about wealth and poverty written by a scholar who has worked as a Christian organizer among landless peasants in his native land, the Philippines.

Brueggemann, Walter. *The Land: Place as Gift, Promise and Challenge in Biblical Faith*. Philadelphia: Fortress Press, 1977. Paper, $5.95.

The book explores relations between God, people and the land as one prism through which to view and understand the Old Testament and the "kingdom" aspect of the New Testament.

Byron, William. *Toward Stewardship: An Interim Ethic of Poverty, Power and Pollution*. New York: Paulist Press, 1975. Paper, $1.95.

Relates biblical understandings of stewardship to such issues as empowerment of the poor and environmental pollution.

Cesaretti, C.A. *Let the Earth Bless the Lord: A Christian Perspective on Land Use*. New York: Seabury, 1981. $6.95. Available from Winston Press.

This collection of essays helps us to think about land use from a variety of angles and to focus on the question of the values we hold in relation to the land.

Freudenberger, C. Dean. *Food for Tomorrow*. Minneapolis: Augsburg, 1984. Paper, $8.95.

A serious look at the soil and water crisis and a call to the renewal of Biblical covenant by a Christian agronomist.

Granberg-Michaelson, Wesley. *A Worldly Spirituality: The Call to Take Care of The Earth*. New York: Harper & Row, 1984. $12.95.

This book is a serious call to a new theological perspective. It begins with a review of the ecological crisis caused by the approach that the earth is an inert, exploitable resource. The author shows a strong line of biblical thought which calls humanity to a caring relationship with all that God has created.

Hall, Douglas John. *The Steward: A Biblical Symbol Come of Age*. New York: Friendship Press, for the Commission on Stewardship, NCC. 1982. Paper, $7.95.

The author provides a biblical critique of the customary western view of stewardship as a means of financing missions; he sees stewardship as servanthood and caring, as opposed to supporting the conquest of nature and other peoples.

Hart, John. *The Spirit of the Earth: A Theology of the Land*. New York: Paulist Press, 1984. Paper, $8.95.

This is a rich reflection on the history of attitudes towards the land. The global effects and human costs of the misuse of land for the maximization of profit are explored here, as well as current action and thought among church people.

Hessel, Dieter T. *Energy Ethics: A Christian Response*. New York: Friendship Press, 1979. Paper, $4.25.

A collection of essays by concerned Christians on the question of energy in relation to religion, society, morality, politics citizen involvement, human environment and the church.

Jegen, Mary Evelyn and Manno, Bruno V., eds. *The Earth Is The Lord's*. New York: Paulist Press. Paper, $4.95.

Essays on stewardship by fifteen Roman Catholic and Protestant scholars. The ethics of stewardship, reflections on economic theory, agriculture policy, the food/energy/environment triangle, and lifestyle are among the themes treated. For youth and adult study groups and individual reading.

Leopold, Aldo. *A Sand County Almanac*. New York: Oxford University Press, 1949. Paper, $6.95.

A collection of essays on changes in nature over a year as observed by the author on his Wisconsin farm. The book is a clear and eloquent statement of the difference between *seeing* and *understanding* the environment.

Manley, Jim. *Seed Songs of Earth and Spirit*. Education for Christian Life and Mission, National Council of Churches of Christ in the U.S.A., 1983.

Songs selected or written in response to the N.C.C.'s outdoor ministries theme: "Sow Seeds—Trust the Promise." All relate to God, Creation, our place in the world and with each other.

McCollough, Charles and Carol. *Lifestyles of Faithfulness*. St. Louis: Christian Board Publications. Order from CBP Press, Box 179, St. Louis, MO 63166. $5.95.

Along with this resource there are three age-level guides for ages 8-11, 12-14 and 15-18, available at $2.95 each.

McLuhan, T.C. *Touch the Earth*. New York: MacMillan, 1959.

An anthology of the sayings and writings of Native Americans on their relationship to the earth and their kinship with all of nature. Early passages reflect the Indians' willingness to share their possessions with the white settlers; later ones show their anger at perceived treachery and broken promises.

Milbrath, Lester W. *Environmentalists: Vanguard for a New Society*. Albany: SUNY Press, 1984. Paper, $9.95.

This political scientist who has worked with other social scientists in Germany, Australia and England reports that he sees a new set of values emerging in these three western industrial societies, which expresses a widening concern for the environment.

Nelson, Jack A. *Hunger for Justice, the Politics of Food and Faith*. New York: Orbis, 1980. Paper, $7.95.

This book combines biblical themes with a political and economic analysis of the causes of world hunger and of U.S. agricultural and military policies. It offers practical steps toward a healthier food system and a more democratic land tenure system.

Nelson-Pallmeyer, Jack. *Water: More Precious than Oil*. Minneapolis: Augsburg, 1982. Paper, $1.75.

This five-session study is designed to renew respect for water as precious resource and powerful Christian symbol. An effective resource for use in groups or by individuals.

Taylor, Richard. *A Community of Stewards*. Minneapolis: Augsburg, 1982. Paper, $1.75.

A guide for congregational study and action on stewardship and consumption. It is especially useful on energy conservation topics.

Yoder, Robert A. *Seeking First the Kingdom, Called to Faithful Stewardship*. Scottdale, PA: Herald Press, 1983. $4.50.

An excellent call to the "holy disturbance" of being both businessperson and Christian. Discussion questions are included at the end of each chapter.

IN SPANISH

Caravias, José Luis. *Luchar por la Tierra: Inspiraciones bíblicas para las comunidades campesinas* (To Struggle for the Land: biblical inspiration for peasant communities). Centro de Estudios y Publicaciones (CEP), Jirón Lampa 808-Apartado 6118, Lima, Perú. 1983.

Lucha por la Tierra: Lucha por la Vida (Struggle for Land: Struggle for Life). Ensayos de Teología Bíblica. Taller de Teología, Número 12, Año 1983. Comunidad Teológica de México, San Jerónimo 137, México 20, D.F.

AUDIO-VISUAL RESOURCES

Your denominational headquarters may have an audio-visual resources library listing many excellent filmstrips and films on the topics covered in PRO-EARTH.

The following audio-visuals may be obtained from the agencies listed.

* * *

A Void of Desolation? 15 minute filmstrip. Purchase price: $18.95.

The purpose of this filmstrip, which includes cassette and leader's guide, is to help the viewer understand toxic waste and nuclear waste problems in North American communities. Individual and group action is encouraged.

Order from:
Friendship Press Distribution Office
P.O. Box 37844
Cincinnati, OH 45237

* * *

The following films are available from:
UNICEF
Information Division, Room 6581
866 United Nations Plaza
New York, NY 10017
(prices available on request)

Water Means Life.
A film on clean water as a crucial, nurturing element for humankind illustrating UNICEF-supported development efforts.

More Than a Sip of Water.
Slide set about Afghanistan, how the water supply is controlled, stored and distributed to areas in most need.

Water.
A film on protection against water-related diseases in Bangladesh by the use of hand-pumped tubewells.

Lifeblood of the Mountains.
Slide set about the results of Pakistan's test well-drilling, how this has been good news for mountain communities.

The Quest for Water.
Slide set about how well-drilling in the Sudan saves women and children from the drudgery of collecting water.

Journey for Survival. 15 minutes.
The International Drinking Water and Sanitation Decade theme film, dramatizing the problems and potential in providing drinking water and sanitation in developing countries.
United Nations Development Programme
Division of Information, Room DC-1972
One United Nations Plaza
New York, NY 10017
   Ask for printed information too.

Wallsheet with photos and text on the needs and objectives of the International Drinking Water and Sanitation Decade. *Price on request.*
World Health Organization
Division of Public Information
20 Avenue Appia
1211 Geneva 27, Switzerland

21 photosheets with 121 photos and related text on International Drinking Water and Sanitation Decade. $6.25.
Earthscan
10 Percy Street
London W1P 0DR
England

───────────

*Audio-visuals marked with an asterix can be used with participants for whom English is a second language. Many of them are effective without the sound. Before showing the audio-visual, ask the group to think about the questions listed in "Guidance for Using Audio-Visual Resources."

The following films are available from:
EcuFilm
810 12th Avenue South
Nashville, TN 37203
Tel: 1-800-251-4091

*And There Was Morning. 10 minutes. Rental: $14.00.
This film celebrates the creative process by picturing scenes of nature and the flight of birds. Images of the simplicity and beauty of nature are contrasted with scenes of its destruction by circumstances of modern life.

*Ark: Man and His Environment. 20 minutes. Rental: $15.00.
Ark is an allegory. The theme that greed will eventually destroy the ecology of our planet is expressed by a man who attempts to save part of the ecological system. That he fails to do so should stimulate discussion about difficult issues in ecology.

Celebrating Tomorrow's Hope. 22 minutes. Rental: $20.00.
This film probes the human and theological dimensions of ecology. What are the religious dimensions of the ecological question? Is there hope for life on earth? Where does this hope show itself?

Multiply and Subdue. 6 minutes. Rental: $12.50.
A series of visuals in both realistic and surrealistic colors, accompanied by organ music intending to inspire a personal re-examination of our stewardship of God's creation.

*For Your Pleasure. 4 minutes. Rental $10.00.
Using the painting "The Hay Wain," by John Constable, we see a 19th century scene crumble into disrepair, the details slowly changing to correspond to the present. Sightseers disturb the scene's tranquility. The farmer's land is cleared away for a highway. The creek becomes a harbor. The horizon of trees become a city skyline. The clean, spacious country air becomes congested with bridges, expressways, neon signs and the pollution of noise. Even the museum in which the painting hangs becomes swallowed up in an urban squeeze of its own.

*The Gifts. 28 minutes. Rental $20.00.
Lorne Greene narrates this powerful visual commentary on the alteration of the American landscape during the last two centuries. It is the story of beauty and spoiled beauty, of life and death. It is intended to remind us of our responsibility to protect our natural resources.

Homeland. 21 minutes. Rental $20.00.
130 years ago, Chief Seattle addressed the government in response to its intention to buy his people's land. He granted their request with the plea that they love and respect the land as the Indians had. As his words invoke the image of a holy place of beauty and life, we see scenes of this beauty, juxtaposed with land despoiled by people and industry. The words of the plea are perhaps more moving and timely today than they were when the speech was delivered.

Beyond the Next Harvest. 27 minutes. Rental $20.00.
Narrator Norman Cousins outlines recent global developments leading to the current world-wide food shortage and proposes realistic alternatives to mass hunger. Based on an attitude of hope, the film emphasizes global interdependence and commitments, and the fact that hunger is everyone's concern.

Diet for a Small Planet. 30 minutes. Rental $20.00.
How does your diet affect the world food crisis, particularly the protein picture? Frances Lappé and Ellen Ewald, authors of the best-selling book of the same title, discuss nutritious diets that are low in meat consumption and make better use of the earth's limited resources.

The Near Edge. 26 minutes. Rental $28.00.
This documentary film studies the changes in lifestyle of families committed to living in the "global community." They have consciously reduced their consumption in response to the worldwide shortage of food and resources. One group lives communally, another shares a garden, a third family teaches agricultural self-sufficiency in Tanzania.

African Drought. 25 minutes. Rental: $27.00.
This documentary film presents the work of Church World Service in the Sahel area of Africa, which was hit by a severe drought. It demonstrates the magnitude of such a disaster and the significance of the church's response.

Appalachia: No Man's Land. 28 minutes. Rental: $25.00.
A highly personalized account of the effects of coal mining on several communities on the West Virginia/Kentucky border.

Food For All. 60 minutes. Rental, $40.00.
Hugh Downs narrates this documentary exploring the causes of the world food crisis. Filmed on locations in the third world and in the U.S., the story suggests long-range solutions and illustrates the plight of the American family farm. Also highlighted are programs which foster rural economic stability and promote better nutrition through education and family planning.

*Garbage. 10 minutes. Rental: $13.50.
No narration, no dialogue, just garbage! This simple but devastating documentary pictures the mountains of trash commonly discarded by Americans. It shows our careless attitude regarding this wasteful problem.

*Seeing God in Mountain Forest. 11 minutes. Rental, $15.00.
As a family spends a day in a mountain forest they come to see nature as a revelation of God's presence. They feel a sense of responsibility to preserve the beauty which God has created.

*Self-Service. 11 minutes. Rental, $15.00.
In this animated satire of our depletion of the earth's natural resources, a swarm of hungry mosquitoes greedily compete to drain their human victim. Facing dire consequences when the supply is exhausted, they are quick to repent . . . until the next opportunity presents itself.

Women in Appalachia—Just Keep on Climbing (Las Mujeres en los Apalaches—Solo Siguen Subiendo) 69 frames, $7.50.
Five women from Dickenson County, WVa talk about life in Appalachia. Included are filmstrip, cassette and Study Guide. In Spanish or English.
Order from: Lutheran Church Women—Order Desk
2900 Queen Lane
Philadelphia, PA 19129

Guidance For Using Audio-visual Resources

In order to link the viewing of these resources with the principle themes of PRO-EARTH, try some of these suggestions. Tell the group *why* you are viewing this particular resource. Ask them to watch for certain things. Follow up the viewing by sharing insights. Ask:

1. What are the ways that you see interrelatedness?
2. How do you see interdependence?
3. What lifestyle choices are being made?
4. What are ways that individuals can make a difference? What are ways that groups can make a difference? What are ways that institutions can make a difference?
5. How do you see stewardship occurring? How is the concept of "neighbor" directing what is occurring?
6. What is the *probable* outcome of this situation by the year 2000? What are the *possible* outcomes by 2000? What is the *preferable* outcome by 2000?

—Carolyn Hardin Engelhardt

ORGANIZATIONS

(Note: Mention of these organizations does not indicate any evaluation of the program, goals or leadership. It is merely an indication of the variety from which you might want to solicit further information.)

American Indian Environment Council
P.O. Box 7082
Albuquerque, NM 87194

The Cousteau Society
Box 2002, Grand Central Station
New York, New York 10164

Common Cause Nuclear Arms Alert Network Hotline
2030 M Street, N.W.
Washington, D.C. 20036

Environmental Defense Fund
444 Park Avenue South
New York, N.Y. 10061

Federal Emergency Management Agency
Washington, D.C. 20472

The Interfaith Coalition on Energy
1411 Walnut Street, Suite 1004
Philadelphia, PA 19102

Sierra Club
530 Bush Street
San Francisco, CA 94108

State Environmental Improvement Divisions

Solar Lobby
1001 Connecticut Avenue, N.W.
Suite 510
Washington, D.C. 20036

Union of Concerned Scientists
1346 Connecticut Ave., N.W.
Suite 1101
Washington, D.C. 20036

The Wilderness Society
1901 Pennsylvania Avenue, N.W.
Washington, D.C. 20006

THE CHURCHES' ACID RAIN PROJECT

This ad-hoc task force aims to educate church members about acid rain and help them fulfil their role as citizens by taking effective action. The project involves national staff of the American Baptist Church, the Christian Church (Disciples of Christ), the Church of the Brethren, The Presbyterian Church (U.S.A.), the United Church of Christ, the United Methodist Church and the National Council of Churches in the U.S.A., working with regional and state church agencies and secular groups such as the National Clean Air Coalition. An Acid Rain Resource Packet has been prepared to help local church groups get started. It includes facts on acid rain, a legislative update, helpful questions and answers, worship and Christian education materials. Available at $3/copy from The Program Agency—Social Education, PCUSA, 475 Riverside Drive, Room 1101, New York, NY 10115.

ECO-JUSTICE WORKING GROUP

An Eco-Justice Working Group has been formed by the National Council of Churches. Representatives from the various denominations work with non-church organizations to educate people in the areas of clean air (including acid rain), toxic wastes and energy concerns. For more information, contact: Ms. Chris Cowap, National Council of Churches—Division of Church and Society, Room 572, 475 Riverside Drive, New York, NY 10115. Tel: (212)870-2421.